641.5956
ATA

KT-592-151

Simply
Lebanese

Simply Lebanese

Ina'am Atalla

Photographs by
Simon Smith

CLASS	BARCODE	
641.595692 ATA	R89718L0589	
DATE	21 DEC 2007	

SOUTH KENT COLLEGE
ASHFORD LEARNING CENTRE

Garnet
PUBLISHING

Dedicated to my husband

Simply Lebanese

Published by
Garnet Publishing Limited
8 Southern Court, South Street
Reading RG1 4QS, UK
Tel: +44(0)118 959 7847
Fax: +44(0)118 959 7356
E-mail: enquiries@garnet-ithaca.co.uk
Website: www.garnet-ithaca.co.uk

Copyright
Text © Ina'am Atalla 2004
Photographs © Simon Smith 2004

The right of Ina'am Atalla to be identified as author of this work has been asserted by her in accordance with the Copyright, Designs and Patents Act 1988.

All rights reserved. No part of this book may be reproduced in any form or by any electronic or mechanical means, including information storage and retrieval systems, without permission in writing from the publisher, except by a reviewer who may quote brief passages in a review.

First edition 2004

ISBN 1 85964 135 0

British Library Cataloguing-in-Publication Data. A catalogue record for this book is available from the British Library.

Credits
Editor
Emma Hawker

Design and Art Direction
David Rose

Production
Typesetting: Samantha Barden

Photography
Simon Smith
Toby Scott (Assistant)

Printed and bound
in Lebanon by International Press

While every care has been taken in the preparation of this book, neither the author nor the publishers can accept any liability for any consequence arising from the use of information contained herein.

CONTENTS

INTRODUCTION

As a young and inexperienced wife starting married life full of expectations, I was very frustrated by not being able to find an indispensable and practical Lebanese recipe book. Like most mothers, mine too had 'handed down' her special recipes, but because I had a busy schedule, and because some of the required ingredients were not widely available at the time, these recipes were largely impractical for daily meals. It was at this point that I made a vow to compile, at my earliest convenience, a cookery book that would salvage and enhance these handed-down recipes and generally ease the pressure involved in putting a meal together, be it cooking healthily for a family, or just for creating simple dishes that even a newcomer to Lebanese cuisine could manage with effective results.

Having set out that task for myself, I then turned my attention to recreating almost all of the dishes in this book simply by remembering the flavours and tastes required to achieve the desired result. Dedication is always the key to success and luckily it happened within this process; as a housewife, cooking for my family became a procedure and a pleasure.

Opening a Lebanese restaurant was the event in my life that gave me the assurance that energy combined with ability and a natural approach to good taste, as well as good presentation, was the key to professional success in cooking. This is particularly the case with Lebanese cooking, as it is probably one of the most decorative, colourful and fresh ingredient-based cuisines. It is simple yet very elegant in its presentation. All these qualities are represented at different times of the year, as each season is rich with its abundance of fruit and vegetables – although it's true to say that these days, one can get almost all the ingredients required at any time of the year.

Having become involved in running the restaurant, the strict schedule and long hours that this role necessitated meant that I couldn't fulfil the mission I had set out to accomplish – putting together a comprehensive book of Lebanese recipes. But it was never far from my thoughts. Indeed, being in direct contact with my restaurant clients was a constant reminder in itself, because they were interested in the food and enquired often about cookery lessons or a book that they could follow. I made endless promises to come up with something useful. Sometimes I even wrote down a few lines of a recipe that a client had expressed an interest in cooking for a dinner party or some other occasion, and I even offered ideas on how to achieve this easily at home. But I never looked on it as a chore; I enjoyed doing it immensely.

And so at long last, and after several years of serious thinking about what this book should contain, I hope the end result will meet everyone's expectations and that the wait has been worth it. For me it is fulfilling that early vow, clarifying my experiences and those of previous generations – all those pleasurable moments of achievement, emphasis on confidence in my skills, and a passion for food in general and Lebanese cuisine in particular. I hope this book will erase any mystery surrounding Lebanese cooking and that the simple techniques will allow you to prepare these popular dishes. More so than ever, modern equipment such as food processors, grinders, blenders and liquidisers make food preparation simple, and add a new dimension to the cuisine. Added to that is the availability and abundance of ingredients in today's supermarkets and specialist stores.

There are some people who deserve a special mention here as they contributed immensely to the production of this book, whether it was through moral support or assurance, or just by keeping check on my well-being throughout the process of 'running the show', sometimes under the most difficult conditions. My dedications are to three women, successful in their own right, and had it not been for Lebanese food we would never have met.

First is Lorna Strauss, an enthusiastic restaurant client and friend. I remember the first time I met her. It was in the kitchen at the restaurant; she introduced herself to me by inquiring about private lessons. Being too busy to take her seriously then, I thought at least the book might help her.

The second has been another pillar of strength to me, and was also originally a client: Janan Harb. I remember coming up the stairs in the restaurant on one occasion … I could hear a woman enquiring about the chef. She insisted the chef must be a woman as, according to her, she could feel and taste the feminine touch throughout her meal. She wanted to meet me, which was not only a pleasure but also the start of a great friendship.

The third is Anne Bishop. She, too, was originally a client, but more than that she gave up her weekends to sit with me while we compiled the recipes that now make up this book. Having realised that I was so busy I would probably never finish this book on my own, she set herself the task of chaining me to a schedule on Sundays to do something about it. We had great fun and we achieved a lot. To her, and to my other two friends, I am truly grateful.

I hope you enjoy this book. My aim in compiling it has been to enhance the knowledge of the already informed, enlighten the unsure and simplify the approach towards this – for one reason or another – largely undiscovered way of eating. In *Simply Lebanese* I have tried to remove some obstacles, hoping that the message gets through and helps to popularise this style of cooking.

THE IMPORTANCE OF *MEZZE* IN LEBANESE CUISINE

Lebanese *mezze* 'is' Lebanese cuisine; it encapsulates this whole style of cooking in a more convincing way than any other kind of *mezze*. This is because the Lebanese lifestyle is very much reflected in their way of eating *mezze*: the Lebanese people relax and take their time eating their *mezze*. For example, they might linger at breakfast until lunchtime, lunch could spread into afternoon tea, and then dinnertime arrives! The *mezze* food helps create an atmosphere of relaxation so that you take your time eating it. Heavy food makes one want to leave the table straight after consuming it, but Lebanese *mezze* makes one want to carry on eating and savouring.

From the simple salad to the raw meats, from cooked vegetable salad dishes, to the more elaborate hot starters, from finger-licking pastries to different breads, perhaps followed by something grilled and light as a main course, are all light, tasty and very fresh. However, despite the fact that one consumes a lot, *mezze* makes it possible to keep your waistline. On my last visit to Lebanon, I lost weight, although I was eating non-stop. I was in the land of salads, *mezze* salads. Pulses make up for the protein richness of meat and in a much more healthy yet tasty way. Nobody gets as far as the main course if they've eaten *mezze* – if it is offered, it is never consumed. Basically you must choose either *mezze* or a main course, never both unless you want to destroy that contented feeling of having had a full meal with all the essential nutrients without feeling guilty about having over-indulged.

The weather adds to the mood created by *mezze*, and the variety of fruits and vegetables available in such abundance and quality demands creativity for those dishes. No other place in the Middle East has the same atmosphere as the Lebanon – and this atmosphere is complemented by the way the Lebanese approach meal times. They insist on a perfect combination of dishes on the table. A vegetable dish has to be present, and whether it contains five vegetables or twenty, this dish has to be at the centre of the dining table. Pickles are normally served with the vegetable dish, even if they are not for eating, for colour, as the look of the table is vital. Then come the olives, green, black, or both. Lots of fresh herbs should be provided too. No other cuisine cares as much for the presentation of seasonal herbs at the table.

Food in general is a very important part of Lebanese social life. Lebanese people eat when they are happy, they eat when they are sad, during holidays, at picnics, weddings and any kind of celebration. *Mezze* is always on the menu. Of course, the selection of dishes alters according to the occasion and the demand, but it is all *mezze* and all carefully prepared, fresh and seasonal. *Mezze* changes from month to month and sometimes week to week as it all is dependent on availability and freshness is essential.

The more one delves into this way of eating the more one realises that it is an important part of social education. *Mezze* is very social. One doesn't have ten dishes of different *mezze* and then sit and eat them in front of the television. The Lebanese people's attitude to food and their vision of what they want out of a meal created Lebanese *mezze* as we know it today. It is in a class of its own, distinctive, refined yet simple and nomadic in origin in many ways.

We are lucky to have *mezze* in Lebanese cuisine. It certainly makes food challenging and interesting both to prepare as well as eat, within the heavy demands of everyday life.

CONVERSION TABLES

These tables give approximate conversions from imperial to metric. If you prefer to work in metric you may find that you have to adjust, very slightly, some of the measurements given. As a general rule, don't mix your measurements; it's best to stick to either imperial or metric. You can assume that tablespoon or teaspoon measurements are 'level' unless the recipe states otherwise.

Weights		Volume	
½ oz	15 g	½ fl oz	15 ml
1	25	1	25
1½	40	2	50
2	50	3	75
3	75	4	110
4	110	5 (¼ pint)	150
5	150	10 (½ pint)	275
6	175	15 (¾ pint)	400
7	200	1 pint	570
8	225	1¼	700
9	250	1½	900
10	275	1¾	1 litre
12	350	2	1.1
13	375	2¼	1.3
14	400	2½	1.4
15	425	2¾	1.6
1 lb	450	3	1.75
1¼ lb	550	3¼	1.8
1½ lb	700	3½	2
2 lb	900	3¾	2.1
3 lb	1.4 kg	4	2.3
		5	2.8
		6	3.4
		7	4.0
		8 (1 gallon)	4.5

Measurements

¼ inch	0.5 cm
½	1
¾	2
1	2.5
2	5
3	7.5
4	10
6	15
7	18
8	20.5
9	23
11	28
12	30.5

Oven temperatures

Gas mark	°F	°C
1	275	140
2	300	150
3	325	170
4	350	180
5	375	190
6	400	200
7	425	220
8	450	230
9	475	240

A–Z OF TOOLS AND EQUIPMENT

These days, there are many labour-saving devices on the market that make it a great deal easier for the cook, regardless of whether he or she is working at a professional level or simply trying to recreate these recipes at home for family and friends. This list covers items that are used frequently throughout *Simply Lebanese*, but of course, there's absolutely nothing stopping you from improvising with the equipment that you currently have in your own kitchen. If you are looking to expand your range of kitchen tools, you might like to refer to the list of suppliers at the end of this section.

Baking trays

You will need two of these, 2 or 3 inches deep. Always choose heavy, non-stick trays as they retain the temperature better without the risk of the pastry sticking.

Chopping board

Buy as large as you can possibly afford.

Coffee kettle (*Raqui*)

Special coffee kettles are widely available from Arabic delicatessens.

Corer

It's worth investing in a good corer to help you core vegetables and prepare them for stuffing. Corers are available in specialist cookery shops.

Food processor

Food processors make cooking more enjoyable and less of a chore. My advice would be to invest in the most powerful one you can afford. A smaller one would also be an asset for preparing things such as salad dressings.

Frying pans and fryers

A good-quality heavy frying pan to use on top of your cooker will save time and give a better flavour to your food. An electric fryer is very useful for deep-frying. Not only is it safe, but the fact that it has temperature control will give you better results.

Grater

It's always better, I think, to grate your own nutmeg rather than buying it ground. Nutmeg graters, which are very effective and allow you to grate just as much as you need at a time, are widely available.

Griddle

Please see the chapter on 'Grills' for more details.

Grinders

A good quality coffee/nut grinder, widely available, is essential for grinding your own spices. It will give you the best results with the least effort.

Knives

My advice to you would be to invest in the best knives you can afford. They will repay you by being more durable and, with the right care, they are guaranteed to give value for money. For the recipes in *Simply Lebanese* you will mainly require just two knives:

- a 21-inch knife for chopping herbs (especially parsley) and salads; and
- a paring (peeling) knife for small jobs.

If you wish, you could add to these an 18-inch cook's knife, which is multi-purpose. Where another specific type of knife is required, it is mentioned in the recipe.

Knife sharpener

If you take the trouble to invest in good knives, then you should also take the trouble to invest in a good knife sharpener. Keeping your knives in the best condition possible will always pay dividends.

Moulds and rings

A *falafel* mould (see p. 16) can make life easier. These moulds are available in Middle Eastern and speciality shops, and are generally reasonably priced. Rings are useful for pastry cutting and making shapes (especially for something like *Kibbeh bisineyeh* – see p. 145).

Mouli

The mouli may well be old-fashioned, but in my opinion it's still the best tool for blending soups and sieving sauces. They are widely available and reasonably priced.

Pastry brush

This item is extremely useful for brushing items with, for example, oil or melted butter directly before cooking. They are relatively inexpensive. The bristles are either packed in a rounded shape or a flat shape. You may find the flat shape slightly more 'economical'.

Skewers

Metal skewers are useful for barbecuing or grilling meat and kebabs. You can buy two types of metal skewer:

- those that are flat and quite sharp-edged; and
- those that are corkscrew in shape.

Go for the 'flat' skewers, as these are easier for threading on your meat and other ingredients. Wooden skewers are also available and are as versatile as metal ones, but cheaper.

Spatulas

These are invaluable for scraping out your pots and pans, bowls and trays. It's best to opt for the rubber heat-resistant variety.

Stockpot with lid

Make sure you have a sturdy pot that has a capacity of at least 2.8 litres (5 pints), which makes boiling a less 'steamy' affair. As well as using your stockpot for cooking, a pot this size can also be used for soaking beans and pulses.

Weights and measures

It doesn't matter whether you weigh your ingredients in imperial or metric, but it is important to stick to one system and make sure that your weighing scales, whatever type, are consistently reliable. You will also need a large jug with volume clearly measured on the side for liquid ingredients. A conversion chart for weights, volume, measurements and oven temperatures is given on pages 10 and 11.

SUPPLIERS

Below is a brief list of outlets for kitchenware and utensils suitable for the preparation and serving of recipes in *Simply Lebanese*. If you are having problems sourcing something locally that you need, it may be as well to phone one of these numbers to see if they can supply it. For those of you that have access to the Internet, a search for kitchen supplies (or something similar) may also pay dividends.

Divertimenti

139/141 Fulham Road
London SW3 6SD
Tel: +44(0)207 581 8065   Email: fulhamroad@divertimenti.co.uk
Fax: +44(0)207 823 9429   Website: www.divertimenti.co.uk

Hansens

Chefs' shop
306 Fulham Road
London SW10 9ER
Tel: +44(0)207 351 6933   Email: sales@hansens.co.uk
Fax: +44(0)207 351 5319   Website: www.hansens.co.uk

Pages Catering Equipment

121 Shaftesbury Avenue
London WC2H 8AD
Tel: +44(0)207 565 5959

Scott & Sargeant Cookshop

24–26 East Street
Horsham
West Sussex
Tel: +44(0)1403 265386   Email: info@internetcookshop.com
Fax: +44(0)1403 210033   Website: www.internetcookshop.com

A–Z OF ESSENTIAL INGREDIENTS

Throughout the range of recipes in this book you'll come across a handful of essential ingredients that give Lebanese cuisine its definable quality, taste and style. When I first started thinking about this collection of recipes, some of the foods and spices mentioned in the list below were difficult to come by. But it's true to say that, these days, many supermarkets will stock most of what you will need to recreate the dishes in *Simply Lebanese*. Additionally, the many specialist delicatessens that have opened in recent years may well be able to provide you with items that supermarkets don't regularly stock. And just to help you, at the end of this section I have included a list of food suppliers who will be able to help you if all else fails.

On a cautionary note, may I urge you to check sell-by and use-by dates on the produce that you buy. Freshness of a product is key to its flavour. And even with dried and canned produce, you will achieve better results if the items are well within the sell-by dates printed on the packaging.

In addition to the essential ingredients listed here, Lebanese cooking utilises a handful of basic combinations of food and spices to make pastes, dips, sauces and accompaniments that are used as part of many of the recipes in this book. Several of these basic items can be made in advance and stored. Full ingredient listings and methods for preparing these are given in the chapter entitled 'Preparing the basics' (pp. 30–49).

Allspice (*bhar hilo*)

Allspice has a hint of cloves, cinnamon and nutmeg. It is a great enhancement to almost all recipes, savoury and sweet, as long as the quantities used are compatible to the flavour required for each individual recipe. The best results can be obtained by freshly grinding the whole grain. Translated from Arabic, *bhar* means 'pepper' and *hilo* means 'sweet'.

Almonds (*lauz*)

These are often used, blanched and split, and are widely available in these forms. They are normally sautéed in clarified butter to be browned slightly before adding to rice and many other dishes.

Broad beans, fresh and dried

Fresh broad beans are available for a very short time each year and do give a good flavour to stews, salads or rice dishes. However dried, split broad beans are also used in Lebanese cooking. Once soaked, they can be minced or ground and are used particularly in making *Falafel* (see pp. 89–91).

Burgul, brown and white

This is a wheat product available in cooked, ground form. It can have either a coarse or a fine texture, and can be white or brown. Brown burgul has a nuttier flavour than white, which is more versatile and starchy. Both forms are used for salads or in making the famous *Kibbeh* (see chapter on *Mezze*: Meat Dishes) in all its forms, and as an accompaniment to casseroles and stews or as a dish on its own. Burgul is truly wholesome and healthy.

Cardamom (*hab-hal*)

Cardamom in used in the Middle East to flavour a variety of dishes. It is most effective when freshly ground. It works particularly well in soups, rice dishes and sauces. In powder form it is added to Arabic coffee. Whole pods are used for flavouring stocks and sauces, and for more old-fashioned recipes.

Cashew nuts

Throughout this book you'll find recipes that use cashew nuts that have been quickly fried in oil, then drained so that they turn a light brown colour.

Chickpeas

Chickpeas are widely available in two forms: in packets dried, or in cans cooked and ready to use. For best results, I prefer dried chickpeas which have been soaked and cooked. You will then have ready the essential ingredient for *Perfect hommous* (see p. 66), a nourishing dip full of energy supplements that is definitely worth making.

Chillies, chilli powder, fresh green chillies and fresh red chillies (*harr*)

In powder form chilli can be overpowering, so it pays to use it sparingly and with caution – especially when preparing marinades or spicy condiments. Fresh green chillies are relatively mild. They are an essential vegetable served as an accompaniment to any meal, and are commonly used for pickling. Red chillies, which are hotter, are generally used to create chilli sauces, chilli pickles and for spicy dishes rather than as an essential table accompaniment.

Cinnamon, powder and sticks (*irfe'*)

In powder form, cinnamon is very versatile. However, it requires moderate use as it can be sometimes be overpowering in savoury dishes. It is particularly flavoursome in puddings. In stick form, it is used for stocks and to flavour sauces.

Coriander, seeds and fresh (*kuzbara*)

As a ground spice, coriander has great versatility. However, the seeds can be quite bland unless they are roasted whole, then ground in a pestle and mortar or a grinder. Make sure you don't overload the grinder, and that you grind the shells and pods evenly. This ground coriander can then be stored in an airtight jar. Coriander is also available ready-ground. As a fresh herb, coriander is irreplaceable, especially in Arabic stews, casseroles, salads and various other dishes with an ethnic influence. It is available nearly all year round, and can be chopped and frozen in polythene bags without losing its flavour for use when needed.

Cumin (*kamoun*)

This is a real delight of a spice. It is excellent with lamb, chicken, fish or any recipe requiring a spicy combination. Its powder form, which is the most commonly available, is also of excellent quality.

Foul

Foul (a small, brown kidney-shaped bean that comes from Turkey or Egypt, which is soaked then cooked) is a very nutritious source of vitamins and protein, and is thus used as a meat alternative for vegetarians. *Foul medamas* (see p. 81) is served mainly as a breakfast dish, but it can be a great energy booster at any time throughout the day. Egyptian *foul* is of the best quality. Always check the sell-by date on the packet to ensure freshness.

Freekeh

Freekeh is from the wheat family, but is not a very well-known ingredient. It is a grain that can be added to soups or an accompaniment to chicken or meat with casseroles and stews. It is flavoursome, healthy and very nutritious. It is widely available in Middle Eastern grocers; the best variety is the toasted, coarse kind, which is much tastier than the finer variety. Look out for it as it is a great item to have in the larder.

Garlic

Garlic is a vital ingredient for most recipes and should therefore be readily to hand. In preparation for its use, it can be peeled, sealed in a container and placed in the lowest part of the refrigerator. It keeps for a week to ten days.

Ghee (*samneh*)

Ghee is clarified butter. There are two kinds: butter ghee and vegetable ghee. It is preferable to use the former in meat dishes and most sweet dishes and pastries. Vegetable ghee is lighter, and is therefore better for use in stews and rice dishes. Both are available from your supermarket.

Kataifi (*sheeriyeh*)

Kataifi is a very thin pastry similar to vermicelli pasta (see below) but even finer. It is sold in specialist Middle Eastern grocers in packets ready for use in *Usmalliyeh* (see p. 201) and various sweets. It can be stored frozen and then defrosted when needed.

Lemons (*leimoun*)

Lemons are essential for the Lebanese kitchen and are used in most dressings, stews and stocks. It is particularly important for flavour that freshly squeezed lemon juice is used.

Lentils (*a'adas*)

Lentils are widely available in many colours and grains, but I have tried to limit their use in this book to just two kinds: red lentils (the smaller version, required mostly for soups and sauces) and whole green lentils (for rice accompaniments and savoury dishes).

Mint, fresh and dried (*n'ana'*)

Different kinds of mint give different results. Mild, fine mint is more suitable for salads, tea and for drying. Mint is excellent in dried form, as long as it is dried naturally. This is done by cutting the stalks and leaves roughly on a tray, allowing them to dry out completely, then rubbing the dried mint through a wide colander, so that it can be collected and sealed in a jar for later use.

Nutmeg (*joset-el-teib*)

Nutmeg loses its flavour very quickly after being grated. The best way of ensuring you get its full flavour is to grate what you need when you need it. Available in powder form also, but the results are not so good.

Oils (*zeit*)

Olive oil: can be used for stews and casseroles.

Extra virgin olive oil: vital for salads and preparing cold vegetable dishes. The better the quality, the better the result.

Other: corn oil is a cheaper and lighter alternative to olive oil. However, it is not so good an alternative for shallow frying as it doesn't get to the required temperature as quickly as olive oil.

Olives, black and green (*zeitoun*)

Black olives are best stored in jars in olive oil. Green olives are washed, then pickled in salty water and lemon juice. Both varieties are used throughout the year as an accompaniment to any meal in the Middle East and in many households as a staple food.

Onion seeds (*habet el barakeh*)

Onion seeds are used in baking (they add great nuttiness to bread) and in pickling goat's cheese in salty water. They are a healthy spice, and, it is said, are good for the heart.

Orange blossom water (*mazaher*)

Orange blossom water is widely available and is essential for puddings and flavouring. Known also as 'white coffee' (*ahwey baida*), it can be added to boiling water to make either an excellent digestive drink after a heavy meal or a great morning starter.

Paprika (*filfil helou*)

Paprika is a mild spice with a great flavour and is a must for marinating chicken or fish, or adding to your cooking to improve the overall taste. As well as the more widely available paprika (which is generally the best kind to use), you can also get a smoked version. But be careful with this, because it can often be overpowering.

Parsley, fresh and dried (*bakdounis*)

Parsley is known as the Queen of Herbs. Flat leaf parsley is more commonly used in Lebanese cuisine, especially for making *Tabbouleh* (see pp. 70–1). The best way to store parsley to maximise on its flavour is to chop it fresh, then keep it in polythene bags in the freezer. Dried parsley can be bland so it's always best to use fresh if you can.

Pepper, black and white (*bhar aswad* and *abiad*)

Black pepper is best obtained as peppercorns and ground straight from the pepper mill as required. White pepper is milder, particularly in ground powder, and is a more delicate enhancer.

Pickles (*kabis*)

Pickles are a vital accompaniment to any Lebanese meal. A variety of food such as carrots, turnips, cauliflower, green chillies, aubergines and especially gherkins or cucumbers, are pickled and used (see pp. 40–4).

Pine nuts (*snoubar*)

Pine nuts are an essential garnish for Lebanese food. To get the maximum flavour, lighly sauté the pine nuts in ghee or clarified butter for a few seconds. The nuts can then be drained and dried on a clean, dry cloth, and set aside in a jar for decorative and other uses.

Pistachios (*foustok halabi*)

Pistachios are widely available. They are best bought shelled, then ground when required and are used especially for decoration in sweets or puddings.

Pomegranates (*roumman*)

Sweet pomegranates are widely available in stores and supermarkets. The small seeds are used to enhance salads and as a topping for fruit and puddings. Sour pomegranates are used for pickling and for making *Dibs al roumman*: syrup. The process involves boiling the juice of the sour pomegranate, which reduces it to a very dark syrupy consistency. Pomegranate syrup (available in Middle Eastern grocers) is great for many recipes and is important in Arabic cooking. It is used as an ingredient in many recipes in this book.

Rice (*ruz*) for savoury and sweet dishes

Generally speaking, there are two types of rice that are used in Lebanese recipes. The first is long grain rice such as basmati. When cooked the grains separate easily. This kind of rice is required for accompaniment rice dishes such as plain boiled rice (see p. 32). Short grain rice, or pudding rice as it is also known, is rounder in shape. When cooked it becomes quite sticky in texture, which makes it ideal for puddings or savoury stuffings.

Saffron (*usfur*)

Saffron is known as the diamond of all spices. In the Middle East, saffron can be bought cheaply in markets as petals picked off the stalks and dried naturally in the sun. The dried petals can then be ground for a finer finish – this will create an overall colour in sauces, stocks and rice dishes.

Salt (*maleh*)

Table salt can be used as a standard base note in Lebanese dishes, while the use of more flavoursome sea salt is recommended for salads and cold dishes.

Sesame seeds (*sumssum*)

Sesame seeds are essentially used as a topping for special breads and with thyme (see below) as a pizza topping and sandwich filling. Toasting them gives maximum flavour.

Semolina (*smeed*)

Semolina is corn meal grain flour. It is either used fine or coarse for puddings and in sweet recipes.

Sumac

Available from Middle Eastern grocers, sumac is made from brown berries harvested at the end of the summer. These berries are left to dry naturally, then ground and sifted. Sumac combines a sour lemon taste with a unique maroon colour, giving height to any recipe – be it a salad, sauce, marinade or simply by adding flavour to a bland ingredient.

Tahini (*tehineh*)

Tahini is basically sesame cream, obtained through a manufacturing process from sesame seeds. It is used in a variety of dips, salads and sauces throughout the Middle East. The best version of tahini is produced in Syria or Lebanon. Dark tahini is not as good as the light-coloured kind as it is heavier and not as creamy when mixed with water and lemon juice. Also, you should always check the sell-by date on the container. Tahini that is not fresh can separate, and is not as tasty and as easy to handle. Always shake the container before use to blend the oils together.

Tamarind (*tamar hindi*)

Literally translated, *tamar hindi* means 'dates from India'. Originally, the main source of tamarind was India, but now it is often imported from Indonesia. It is widely available in paste form, which is very versatile and useful, and is the type I prefer to use. Alternatively, it can be bought dried, which means that before use it needs to be soaked, blended and sieved. Tamarind is essential in Arabic cooking, especially for sauces and stuffed vegetable dishes, as it adds an edge and body to the recipes.

Thyme, fresh and dried (*za'atar achdar*)

Fresh thyme is a winter/early spring herb and a seasonal delicacy. The Lebanese variety is more flavoursome than the European or Italian varieties. However, it is rarely available outside of Lebanon, because its delicacy (particularly the green type) means that it can't withstand changes of temperature. In flavour the Lebanese version is like a combination of rocket leaves, oregano and thyme, and is a subtle addition to all dishes, hot or cold. Commercially, dried Lebanese thyme is mixed with other spices such as sumac and toasted sesame seeds, and sold in powder form to be used in *Manakeesh* (see pp. 218–19) or simply as a dip with olive oil for sandwiches, making it part of one of the best snacks in the Middle East. Thyme is best used fresh. However, it can be taken off its stalks, dried naturally on a large tray, then ground either coarsely or semi-coarsely and kept in airtight jars. *Zeit wa za'atar* (olive oil and thyme) is an essential breakfast item in any household around the Mediterranean.

Vermicelli (*sheeriyeh*)

Vermicelli is pasta made into very long, thin strands. It is widely available, and used for rice accompaniments and some puddings.

Vinegar (*khal*)

Malt vinegar is essential for pickles, while white wine vinegar is used for marinades and dressings.

Vine leaves (*warak inab*)

It is very difficult to find fresh vine leaves. However pickled vine leaves have greatly improved in recent times. You can also buy the leaves dried, in packets or glass jars. See p. 49 for preparation.

Walnuts (*j'ose*)

The better quality walnut you use, the better the results in cooking. For most recipes, walnuts need to be coarsely ground. The best results can be obtained by pulsing them (either raw, fried or toasted) in a food processor.

SUPPLIERS

Below is a brief list of food suppliers.

Archies Foodstore

14 Moscow Road

London W2 4BP

Tel: +44(0)207 229 2275

Damas Gate Food Wholesalers

81 Uxbridge Road

London W12 8NR

Tel: +44(0)208 743 5116

Green Valley

36 Upper Berkeley Street

London W1H 7PG

Tel: +44(0)207 402 7385

Haddad Food Store

121–123 Chiswick High Road

London W4 2ED

Tel: +44(0)208 995 4547

La Belles Boucherie

3 Bell Street

London NW1 5BY

Tel: +44(0)207 258 0230

Middle East Food Market

383 Uxbridge Road

London W3 9SA

Tel: +44(0)208 752 0678

The Nutcase Ltd (for coffee and nuts)

352 Uxbridge Road

London W12 2LL

Tel: +44(0)208 743 0336

Rayan (for sweets)

Unit B24

7–11 Minerva Road

Park Royal

London NW10 6HJ

Tel: +44(0)208 537 9033

PREPARING THE BASICS

Throughout the recipes in *Simply Lebanese* – and in Lebanese cooking in general – you'll come across a handful of frequently used accompaniments: sauces, dips, dressings and side dishes. These basics contribute to the unique style that is Lebanese cuisine – and the real beauty of them is that many can be made in advance and stored.

Ruz abiad

SERVES: **4**

PREPARATION TIME: **10 minutes**

COOKING TIME: **15 minutes**

1 tablespoon ghee, or clarified butter, or 50 ml (2 fl oz) corn oil

450 g (1 lb) basmati rice, soaked in 570 ml (1 pint) boiling water for 5 minutes, then drained, rinsed under hot running water, then drained again in a colander

1 teaspoon salt

700 ml (1¼ pints) boiling water

TEMPERATURE
preheat the oven to gas mark 5, 375°F (190°C)

YOU WILL ALSO NEED
a heavy, medium-sized ovenproof pot, with lid, 22 cm (9 inches) in diameter

White rice

Plain white rice is the most basic of foods and one of the most versatile and simple to cook. It is a basic accompaniment to so many dishes. It is important to decide what type of rice you will be using. I recommend basmati, which is widely available and excellent quality. It also behaves well on reheating – especially in a microwave. Once you have mastered this recipe, you will have learned a vital skill.

1 Heat the ghee, butter or corn oil in the pot. When hot, add the drained rice, turning gently on a high heat for a few minutes to coat each grain and heat through.

2 Once the rice starts to make a noise, add the salt and then the boiling water.

3 Stir once, lower the heat, and leave the rice to simmer until most of the water is absorbed.

4 Put the lid on, or cover with foil, and transfer to the heated oven. Leave to finish cooking for a further 5 minutes.

5 The rice is ready when you can see tiny holes in the cooked rice. Take out of the oven and serve.

TIPS

- Rice does not need a deep pot or pan, but the pot or pan needs to be wide enough to cook the rice evenly.
- Always use boiling water for soaking and cooking the rice.
- Do not stir the rice while it is cooking as this causes the grains to stick together and not separate as required.
- Stir the rice gently when it comes out of the oven before serving it.
- Allow the rice to stand (if possible) for a few minutes before serving.
- Cover any leftover rice and refrigerate. To re-heat, use the microwave.

Croutons

These are small squares of bread that are deep-fried in vegetable oil. They can be used with salads and soups or as an optional decoration for a variety of other dishes. You can also make toasted croutons. Both kinds have their own individual characteristics which define their use. I prefer to use fried croutons for winter dishes and toasted for summer salads. A different kind of bread is used for each.

FOR THE FRIED CROUTONS

1 Fry the pieces of bread in three batches to ensure the croutons cook quickly and brown evenly.

2 When the croutons are light brown in colour, lift them on to a dry cloth or absorbent kitchen paper, and leave them to drain and cool.

TIPS

• When kept dry, croutons can stay fresh for 3–4 weeks.

• Croutons can be stored in an airtight tin, which will keep them crispy until needed.

FOR THE TOASTED CROUTONS

1 Place the pieces of pitta bread on the baking tray and then place under the grill, toasting them for 2 minutes. Then shake the tray and toast them for another minute.

2 Switch off the grill and leave the croutons to finish toasting and to become crisp for a further 2 minutes or so.

3 Remove from the grill and allow to cool. When cold, store in an airtight container for use when required.

TIPS

• The size and shape of the pitta pieces can be varied according to personal taste.

• The croutons have to be crisp and cold before they are stored away.

• The thinner the pitta bread, the lighter and more crisp the croutons.

• The quantity above is enough for 2–3 weeks, although it is better to make croutons as you need them: the fresher the better.

• This kind of crouton is ideal for adding to salads or as a topping for soups.

PREPARATION TIME: **15 minutes**

COOKING TIME: **10 minutes**

FOR THE FRIED CROUTONS
a small white or brown sliced loaf, cut into 1 cm cubes

TEMPERATURE
preheat the deep fryer to 325°F (180°C)

FOR THE TOASTED CROUTONS
2 pitta breads, opened up and cut into 2 cm cubes

TEMPERATURE
preheat the grill to its highest setting

Home-made yoghurt

SERVES: **4–5**

PREPARATION TIME: **20 minutes**

PROVING TIME: **6–8 hours plus minimum 2 hours chilling time**

1.1 litres (2 pints) full-cream milk
110 ml (4 fl oz) plain set yoghurt

YOU WILL ALSO NEED
a glass or plastic container with a lid

There is an abundance of prepared plain yoghurts on the market these days and many of them are perfectly good enough to use in the recipes in this book. However, I like to think that nothing beats the taste of home-made yoghurt. And nothing gives you greater satisfaction than knowing you have prepared it yourself.

1 Heat the milk to boiling point, then set aside to cool.

2 Test the temperature with your finger; it needs to have cooled down enough to touch, i.e. body temperature.

3 Put the yoghurt in a small bowl and gently add enough of the boiled milk to blend it into a thick liquid form. Then, more swiftly, add the rest of the milk.

4 Transfer the mixture to a waiting container. Put the lid on, cover with a couple of clean kitchen cloths and put in a warm place for a minimum of 6–8 hours.

5 Move to the refrigerator and chill for a minimum of 2 hours.

TIPS

• The time for proving will vary from season to season; it will take less time in the summer and longer in the winter. In fact, leaving it overnight is probably best in winter.

• Do not shake the yoghurt/milk mixture after mixing.

• For creamier and thicker yoghurt, add 2 tablespoons of dried milk to the milk after it has been boiled, mix in well and allow to cool as before.

• The yoghurt can be divided into smaller containers as long as they have lids and are covered well.

Cucumber and yoghurt salad

This salad is probably the most versatile in Lebanese cuisine and it is simple to make and popular. Its ingredients are very basic and available everywhere. Its preparation is quick and easy, and once it is prepared it can be kept in the refrigerator without losing any of its quality. It is a great accompaniment to many meals and snacks: as a dip this salad is a great asset of Lebanese mezze, and with rice dishes it is irreplaceable. Good ingredients always result in a great dish, and this is especially true here. Quality yoghurt is a must, as are fresh cucumbers.

1. In a medium-sized bowl, mix the chopped cucumber, yoghurt, salt and garlic (if used) until well blended.

2. Cover and chill in the refrigerator until needed.

3. To serve, sprinkle with the dried or fresh mint.

TIPS

- The salad can be prepared well in advance, layered in a bowl ready to mix together when needed. (Layering it prevents it from going soggy.)

- The quality of the yoghurt used determines the consistency of the salad. Personally I prefer a thicker version as the salad creates its own juices while waiting in the refrigerator; the thicker version also has a longer life.

- Garlic enhances the salad, but use sparingly so as not to overpower the other basic flavours.

2 small cucumbers (or ½ large cucumber), peeled and evenly chopped

275 ml (10 fl oz) *Home-made yoghurt* (see p. 34) or other plain yoghurt

½ teaspoon salt

1 clove garlic, peeled and finely chopped (optional)

TO GARNISH
½ teaspoon dried or 1 teaspoon chopped fresh mint

Kouzbara wa toum

MAKES: **175–225 g (6–8 oz)**
PREPARATION TIME: **20 minutes**
COOKING TIME: **10 minutes**

2 tablespoons vegetable ghee or
clarified butter

6 cloves garlic, peeled and
finely chopped

2 bunches coriander, finely chopped

YOU WILL ALSO NEED
a jar or a plastic container with a lid

Coriander and garlic paste

This really is the 'king' of standby pastes. When made it can be kept in an airtight container or jar and stored in the refrigerator. The paste can be spread on lamb steaks, fish or chicken prior to cooking. A teaspoonful or two (according to your taste) makes a great addition to stews, and to a variety of other sauces and dressings.

1 Heat the ghee or butter in a frying pan, and while it is heating add the garlic. Stir the garlic round to cook it through gently without browning.

2 Lower the heat and add the chopped coriander. Mix well with the garlic for a minute or so.

3 At this stage, turn off the heat. Pour the mixture into the waiting container and allow to cool.

4 When cold, cover the container and place in the refrigerator until needed.

TIPS
• Don't wait for the ghee or butter to get hot before you add the garlic to it, otherwise the garlic browns before it cooks and discolours the ghee or butter and then the paste.

• The secret of retaining the colour of the coriander is to add the coriander to the garlic just as it starts to cook, and then mix them together for a very short time; then take them off the heat to cool. Essentially you are sautéeing them to capture the heat.

Garlic sauce

This sauce is used particularly for grills. It is indispensable as it provides the base for successful grill dishes. It is also an important dip for authentic Lebanese mezze. It complements raw meats such as Kafta nayyeh, Habra nayyeh and of course the famous Kibbeh nayyeh. Once made, it can be kept for up to 6 weeks in the coldest part of the refrigerator. Remember to use it sparingly as it is very powerful. My version is extremely straightforward; the key to its success is to use very fresh ingredients.

1 Place the cloves of garlic and salt in a food processor. Process until the garlic is puréed.

2 Once the garlic is puréed, add the potato pieces through the feed tube of the food processor one by one, making sure that they are puréed and blended with the garlic.

3 Drip the corn oil slowly through the feed tube, so that the ingredients begin to form a mayonnaise-like consistency.

4 When all the oil has been used, add the lemon juice through the tube.

5 When the sauce thickens, switch off the processor. Transfer the mixture to an airtight container and store in the coolest part of the refrigerator.

TIPS

• Traditionally, eggs are used instead of potatoes but this method is just as tasty and keeps for longer.

• The garlic should be very fresh and only peeled just before preparation for best results and a fuller flavour.

• The slower you drip the oil through the feed tube, the better the result.

• Store the sauce in the base of the refrigerator in an airtight container. This way it will keep for 4–6 weeks.

Toum

MAKES: **570 ml (1 pint)**
PREPARATION TIME: **30 minutes**

12 cloves garlic, peeled

1 teaspoon salt

1 medium potato, peeled and diced

300 ml (12 fl oz) corn oil

25 ml (1 fl oz) lemon juice

YOU WILL ALSO NEED
an airtight container

Green chilli dip

PREPARATION TIME: 10 minutes

5 green chillies (medium heat), deseeded

2 cloves garlic, peeled and finely chopped

1 teaspoon salt

1 teaspoon lemon juice

50 ml (2 fl oz) extra virgin olive oil

YOU WILL ALSO NEED
a jar or a plastic container with a lid

This versatile dip is made from a variety of fresh ingredients which are simply blended together and then stored in the refrigerator until needed. It can be used for up to a week. The chillies become milder as they are mixed with the olive oil and lemon juice. It is a great enhancer of any vegetable dish, and is mainly used as a dip for crudités, vegetables eaten before a typical Lebanese meal. It can also be used in the numerous recipes where chilli is needed for a spicy effect, or where green chillies are required.

1 Place the chillies in a food processor and process for a few seconds.

2 Transfer the chillies to a bowl, add the chopped garlic, salt, lemon juice and olive oil. Mix well.

3 Transfer to the container or jar, place in the refrigerator and serve when needed.

TIPS
* If a processor is not available, chop the garlic and the chillies finely and mix in the rest of the ingredients. Wear gloves for chopping the chillies, if possible.

* Keep the dip covered at all times. If it starts to dry out just add more olive oil. This will also help retain the colour of the dip.

Red chilli sauce

PREPARATION TIME: 20 minutes

5 red chillies (medium heat), deseeded

½ red pepper, deseeded and roughly chopped

2 cloves garlic, peeled

½ teaspoon granulated sugar

1 teaspoon salt

½ teaspoon white pepper

1 teaspoon Dijon mustard

Once made, this hot, spicy sauce can be chilled until required. Its uses are numerous: it can be used as a dip with crudités or mixed with various sauces to subtly perk them up – instant magic!

1 Into a food processor place the red chillies, red pepper, garlic, sugar, salt, pepper, mustard, Tabasco, tomato ketchup, tomato purée and olive oil.

2 Process these ingredients together until well mixed and blended and until the mixture turns into a thick sauce.

3 Transfer into the airtight container and place in the refrigerator until it is needed.

TIPS
- It is essential that the container is airtight in order to prolong the life of the sauce.
- The sauce keeps for up to 3–4 weeks, if kept well chilled in the refrigerator.

1 tablespoon Tabasco

4 tablespoons tomato ketchup

½ tablespoon tomato purée

175 ml (6 fl oz) extra virgin olive oil

YOU WILL ALSO NEED
an airtight container

Turnip pickle

PREPARATION TIME: **30 minutes**

WAITING TIME: **1 week – 10 days**

1.4 kg (3 lb) raw turnips (choose evenly sized, firm and fresh turnips)

225 g (8 oz) raw beetroot, sliced

3 green chillies, deseeded and roughly chopped

1.75 litres (3 pints) cold water

75 g (3 oz) salt

25 g (1 oz) granulated sugar

570 ml (1 pint) red wine vinegar

YOU WILL ALSO NEED
a pickling jar of 2.3 litre (4 pint) capacity, with a tight lid

The Lebanese dining table always has kabis on it because pickles are an essential accompaniment to any Lebanese meal. The abundance of varieties of pickles available in supermarkets and delis could be said to make the effort of making them at home seem unnecessary and time-consuming. Nevertheless, personally I prefer to make my own pickles (particularly turnip pickles), as bought pickles are never as fresh and crunchy as the home-made variety. Another thing that worries me about commercially made pickles are the additives and enhancers they contain. All in all, if you have time, I would advise you to make your own, as the whole exercise is very simple. The photograph on p. 41 shows you the impressive finished result.

1 Wash the turnips and leave them whole.

2 Layer the turnips, beetroot and chillies in your pickling jar.

3 In a bowl, mix together the water, salt and sugar and stir very well to dissolve the salt and sugar in the mixture.

4 Add the vinegar, stir to blend in and pour the mixture onto your layered vegetables in the pickling jar.

5 Seal the jar tightly and allow the pickles to mature in a cool, dry place away from direct heat for at least a week before eating.

TIPS
- The quality of the turnips will determine the result.
- Red wine vinegar is not as sharp as malt vinegar and a mixture of the two is good. However, using just red wine vinegar improves the shelf life of the pickles.
- When taking pickles out of the jar, make sure that a) a clean utensil is used, and b) the jar is tightly resealed.
- A tight lid and seal on the pickling jar is very important; the pickles will become soft otherwise.
- The effect of the chillies will be minimal, so don't worry about them. They are used it to enhance the pickles' flavour.

1.6 kg (3½ lb) small evenly sized
cucumbers

3 green chillies, deseeded and halved

3 cloves garlic, peeled and halved

1.6 litres (2¾ pints) cold water

75 g (3 oz) salt

25 g (1 oz) granulated sugar

275 ml (½ pint) white wine vinegar

YOU WILL ALSO NEED
a pickling jar of 3.4 litre (6 pint)
capacity, with a tight lid

Cucumber pickle

This pickle is just as easy as the previous recipe. The only difficulty lies in the availability of the right size of cucumbers. The cucumbers should be small and very fresh, not long and wilted. They are not easy to find, as the season for them is quite short, being late spring and early to mid summer, so my advice is to buy them during that period and pickle a few batches. As long as the jars are well sealed, and kept in a cool place, the pickles will last and be as good as when you first made them.

1   Wash the cucumbers and using a knife prick the middle of each one.

2   Layer the cucumbers neatly in the jar, interspersing the layers with the chillies and garlic slices.

3   In a bowl, mix together the water, salt and sugar and stir well to dissolve the salt and sugar.

4   Add the vinegar, stir to blend in, and pour into the pickling jar.

5   Seal the jar tightly and allow the pickles to mature in a cool, dry place away from direct heat for at least a week before eating.

TIPS

*   Green chillies can replaced by sweet peppers if a milder version is required.

*   When layering the cucumbers in the jar do not apply too much pressure.

*   When taking the pickles out of the jar, make sure that a) a clean utensil is used and b) the jar is tightly resealed.

1 large cauliflower, separated into
individual florets

225 g (8 oz) raw beetroot, sliced
(optional)

Cauliflower pickle

This is another version of pickle that is very straightforward and easily made. Cauliflower is available all year round, and it is easy to find quality ones so you have no excuse not to try making it!

1   Put the cauliflower florets in the pot of water, bring the water to the boil on a moderate heat, then quickly immerse the cauliflower florets in the bowl of cold water.

2 Transfer the florets to a colander and wash under cold running water for few minutes to cool them down further.

3 Layer the cauliflower with the beetroot (if used) and chillies in the pickling jar neatly without applying pressure.

4 In a bowl, mix the water, salt and sugar and stir to mix and dissolve.

5 Add the red wine vinegar, mix in, then pour into the pickling jar.

6 Seal the jar tightly, and allow the pickle to mature in a cool, dry place away from direct heat for a week before eating.

TIPS
• Cooked beetroot (whole) can be used instead of raw beetroot. It gives the pickle a lovely pink colour.

• Do not over-blanch the cauliflower as it will reduce its crunchiness.

• The effect of the chillies will be minimal, so don't worry about them. They are just used to enhance the flavour.

• When taking the pickles out of the jar, make sure that a) a clean utensil is used, and b) the jar is tightly resealed.

Aubergine pickle

I have inherited this recipe from my mother. Being a very good 'pickler', my mother used to pickle everything. She never could make a cake, but pickles were her speciality. I was brought up on this aubergine pickle. We always had it on our dining table accompanying a meal. We mixed it with tomatoes to make salads, ate it with cheese, meat, chicken – in fact, just about everything. It is not the simplest pickle to make, but once tried, it becomes easy. It is especially good for summer, as it is full of flavour and summer freshness. You must use special aubergines: the kind required are small and thin, used only for pickling. You can buy them from Middle Eastern grocers and supermarkets. They are seedless, sweeter than the normal aubergine and very mild in flavour. Their shape is very inviting, but as usual make sure that they are very fresh and not wilted.

2 green chillies, deseeded and roughly chopped

1.4 litres (2½ pints) cold water

75 g (3 oz) salt

25 g (1 oz) granulated sugar

400 ml (¾ pint) red wine vinegar

YOU WILL ALSO NEED
a large pot filled with 2.3 litres (4 pints) cold water

a large bowl filled with cold water

a pickling jar of 3.4 litre (6 pint) capacity, with a tight lid

Kabis bitinjan

PREPARATION TIME: 40 minutes
WAITING TIME: 1 week – 10 days

1.8 kg (4 lb) small pickling aubergines

½ bunch flat leaf parsley, finely chopped

3 cloves garlic, peeled and finely chopped

1 small red or green chilli, deseeded and finely chopped

½ teaspoon salt

1.75 litres (3 pints) cold water

75 g (3 oz) salt

1 tablespoon granulated sugar

150 ml (¼ pint) white wine vinegar

YOU WILL ALSO NEED
a large pot filled with 2.3 litres
(4 pints) cold water

a large bowl filled with cold water

a pickling jar of 3.4 litre (6 pint)
capacity, with a tight lid

1 Trim the aubergines, add to the pot of water and put on to heat. Bring to the boil and then simmer the aubergines for roughly 12–15 minutes until they have softened.

2 Test the aubergines and as soon as they are soft, take them off the heat and immerse in the cold water in the bowl so that they cool instantly.

3 Transfer the aubergines to a colander and wash them under cold running water for few minutes, drain and set aside, and allow to cool completely.

4 Meanwhile, mix the chopped parsley, garlic, chilli and salt in a small bowl.

5 Take one cooled aubergine and, using a sharp knife, slit the aubergine from the middle to the end, opening it out to allow for stuffing.

6 Stuff the aubergines with about half a teaspoon of the parsley and garlic mixture and then press the two halves back together. Tidy up the outside so it is free from the stuffing.

7 Repeat with the rest of the aubergines. Layer the aubergines neatly and gently into the pickling jar.

8 In a bowl mix the cold water, salt and sugar and stir to mix and dissolve. Add the wine vinegar, mix in, and then pour into the pickling jar.

9 Seal the jar tightly and allow the pickles to mature in a cool, dry place away from direct heat for at least a week before eating.

TIPS
- This pickle might sound hard work, but it is well worth the effort if you are planning a treat, and if the right kind of aubergines are available.
- Chilli can be replaced by sweet pepper if a milder effect is required.
- Do not overcook the aubergines: the minute they feel soft, take them off the heat and cool.
- The same recipe can be followed without stuffing the aubergines. Cook the aubergines, cool and then layer them in the jar with 3 sliced cloves of garlic, one halved green or red chilli and follow the rest of the recipe.
- When taking the aubergines out of the jar, make sure that a) a clean utensil is used and b) the jar is tightly resealed.

Special salad dressing

This is the most important essential to have in your refrigerator. This popular salad dressing can be stored in an airtight container for use when ready. It is particularly good for dressing a leafy or chunky summer salad.

1 Place all the ingredients in a blender and blend for 1 minute. You could mix the ingredients in a jar, but I find that a blender is more efficient and the dressing does not separate so easily when stored.

2 Store in the refrigerator in an airtight jar.

TIPS
• Garlic can be omitted if you prefer.

• Sesame oil is optional, but try to include it as it adds a fantastic nutty flavour.

• Use the dressing sparingly as it is very flavoursome.

MAKES: **300 ml (½ pint) dressing**

1 clove garlic

1 teaspoon granulated sugar, or honey

1 teaspoon salt

½ teaspoon freshly ground black pepper

50 ml (2 fl oz) red or white wine vinegar

1 tablespoon Dijon mustard (or alternatively an extra tablespoon of red or white wine vinegar)

200 ml (4 fl oz) extra virgin olive oil

1 tablespoon lemon juice

25 ml (1 fl oz) sesame oil (optional)

YOU WILL ALSO NEED
a jar with a screw-top lid

Syrup

Ater, as it is known in Arabic, is the golden syrup of the Middle East. Perfecting it needs experience, but most of all the proportion of the ingredients used should be accurate as this will affect the consistency of the syrup and this in turn will affect any sweet pastry or pudding that it accompanies or seals. Don't worry if this is your first attempt; all you need to do is follow the instructions carefully and you won't go wrong.

1 In a deep pan add the sugar followed by the water, lemon juice and orange blossom water. Mix together.

2 Put the pan on a hob at a low to moderate heat and allow the liquid to simmer for 15 minutes, reducing the heat as it boils gently. The syrup is ready when it has thickened a little and its colour is slightly yellowish.

Ater

MAKES: **570 ml (1 pint) syrup**
PREPARATION TIME: **5 minutes**
COOKING TIME: **15 minutes**

1 kg (2 lb 2 oz) granulated sugar

570 ml (1 pint) cold water

1 tablespoon lemon juice

2 tablespoons orange blossom water (see p. 25)

YOU WILL ALSO NEED
an airtight bottle

3 Cool the syrup. When cold, pour into a glass bottle, seal and use the syrup hot or cold as needed.

TIPS

- For hot syrup, simply pour into a saucepan and reheat gently on a low heat.
- Cold syrup is very versatile, and can be added to milkshakes and fruit smoothies as a sweetener.
- The syrup thickens as it cools but don't worry as this is how it should be.

Tabla

SERVES: **4**

PREPARATION TIME: **20 minutes**

1 white onion, peeled and finely sliced

1 red onion, peeled and finely sliced

1 red pepper, deseeded and finely sliced

2 tablespoons chopped fresh parsley

Tabla is a traditional accompaniment to many dishes. It is a garnish as well as a crunchy salad, and is used as an enhancement to grills and raw meat dishes. It forms the base for various Lebanese salads.

1 Mix all the above ingredients in a bowl and serve as required.

TIPS

- A very sharp knife is needed to achieve the best results, as a blunt knife would bruise the onions and peppers and so reduce the life and freshness of the *Tabla*.
- Kept covered with cling film in the coldest part of the refrigerator, the *Tabla* will keep for 5–6 days.
- *Tabla* can be added to various salads to enhance and add flavour.

Tahini sauce

Taratour, *as this sauce is called in Arabic, is a must-have accompaniment to* Falafel *(pp. 89–91), fried fish and all kinds of grilled food. It is both versatile and simple to make.*

1 In a bowl, mix together the tahini and half the water. Then add the salt and blend.

2 Add the lemon juice, mix, then add the rest of the cold water. Mix. Taste and adjust accordingly.

3 Add the chopped parsley, mix in and pour the tahini sauce into the jar. Chill in the refrigerator until needed.

TIPS

• The quality of the tahini will determine the creaminess of the sauce. Look out for well-mixed tahini that is pale rather than dark.

• Never add the lemon juice first as the sauce will become too thick and will lose its creaminess.

• The sauce will thicken in the refrigerator so always add a bit of water before you use it.

Taratour

MAKES: **300 ml (½ pint)**
PREPARATION TIME: **5 minutes**

150 ml (5 fl oz) tahini

225 ml (8 fl oz) cold water

1 teaspoon salt

75 ml (3 fl oz) lemon juice

1 tablespoon chopped fresh parsley

YOU WILL ALSO NEED
a jar with a screw-top lid

Coriander pesto

This is a very good alternative to the Coriander and garlic paste *on p. 36. It is however more versatile as it can be used as a salad dressing or as an addition to soup, or generally to enhance the flavour of anything that needs lifting. It can be prepared simply in a food processor or blender, and kept in a glass jar in the refrigerator until needed. A great asset in the kitchen.*

1 Place the garlic cloves into a food processor and chop finely.

2 Add the coriander, salt and black pepper. While the machine is on, pour the olive oil gently and slowly through the feed tube of the processor.

3 Taste and adjust seasoning accordingly, pour into a glass jar, screw the lid on tightly and keep in the refrigerator for future use.

MAKES: **275 ml (½ pint) jar**
PREPARATION TIME: **10 minutes**

2 cloves garlic, peeled

1 bunch coriander, finely chopped

220 ml (8 fl oz) extra virgin olive oil

½ teaspoon salt

¼ teaspoon freshly ground black pepper

YOU WILL ALSO NEED
a jar with a screw-top lid

TIPS

- The pesto keeps in the refrigerator for at least a week to 10 days if covered tightly and used carefully.

- The consistency can be determined according to individual taste – add more oil if a more liquid pesto is needed.

- Dijon mustard can be added to the ingredients if a stronger version is preferred.

Preparation of vine leaves

Warak inab literally means 'the paper of the grapes', hence the definition vine leaves. They are probably the most common delicacy in the Middle East, especially as nearly everyone has a vine growing in the garden. The vine leaves are picked on demand and are therefore as fresh as they can possibly be. The quality of the vine leaves as well as their availability encourages the housewife to spend hours of intensive work preparing the leaves for cooking, delighted at the prospect of giving her family and friends a great treat. Vine leaves are enjoyed by everyone, whether vegetarian or not. They are best fresh, and are also good pickled.

1 Blanch the vine leaves in boiling water for a few minutes. In the case of fresh ones, the colour changes from green to a light brown colour. Turn them over while blanching to get an even colouring.

2 Drain, wash under cold running water to cool and then strain through a colander. Set aside until needed.

3 Remove the stalks of the vine leaves before using.

Preparation of chickpeas

In this book, tinned chickpeas can be used but I feel that they do produce a less smooth texture to those that you have soaked and boiled yourself. Prepared chickpeas are an essential ingredient in making Perfect hommous *(see p. 66).*

1 Soak chickpeas overnight in double their quantity of cold water.

2 Drain, then rinse under cold running water.

3 Place the drained chickpeas in a large pot, then cover with cold water. Add ½ teaspoon of bicarbonate of soda. Leaving the pot uncovered, bring the contents to the boil and simmer gently for 20 minutes. Stir every now and again.

4 The chickpeas are cooked when they are tender and their skins come off easily. Remove from the heat, and drain.

5 Wash under running water for at least 5 minutes, tapping gently to help wash off any remaining skins.

SOUPS

Soups are wonderful all-rounders. They can be flavoursome and nutritious. You can eat them as a starter to your main meal or they can be a meal in themselves. They can be warm and comforting and are so simple to make. Served with some warm pitta or toasted bread, or perhaps some croutons or chopped parsley, they are a trouble-free addition to Lebanese cuisine.

All-in-one soup

SERVES: **4–5**

PREPARATION TIME: **20 minutes**

COOKING TIME: **1 hour**

75 ml (3 fl oz) extra virgin olive oil

2 poussins, cleaned and jointed, washed and then dried, or 6 chicken thigh portions

1 medium onion, peeled and finely chopped

1 teaspoon granulated sugar

2 cm (¾ inch) root ginger, peeled and finely chopped

2 cloves garlic, peeled and finely chopped

2 teaspoons salt

½ teaspoon white pepper

½ teaspoon ground coriander

½ teaspoon cumin

1 teaspoon saffron

½ teaspoon cinnamon

½ teaspoon ground allspice

1 teaspoon ground cardamom

1 large carrot, peeled and finely sliced

1 red pepper, deseeded and thinly sliced

2.3 litres (4 pints) boiling water

50 g (2 oz) short macaroni or any small pasta shapes

110 g (4 oz) fresh spinach, roughly chopped (optional)

50 g (2 oz) unsalted butter

25 g (1 oz) fresh coriander, finely chopped

This soup is ideal served on a cold winter's day. It is a meal in its own right, as it is very satisfying and filling. All it needs is some crusty bread or toasted pitta to accompany.

1 Heat a large deep pot. Add the olive oil followed by the poussin or chicken pieces and sauté to brown for 3–4 minutes. Add the onion and sugar and mix in, frying for a further 2 minutes.

2 Add the chopped ginger and garlic followed by the salt, pepper, ground coriander, cumin, saffron, cinnamon, allspice and cardamom and mix well.

3 Sauté together for a minute and then add the carrot and red pepper, mix together, lower the heat and add the boiling water.

4 Cover and allow the mixture to simmer on a moderate heat for 20 minutes. If using chicken, cook for 30 minutes.

5 Add the macaroni (or other pasta) and spinach (optional). Cook for a further 10–15 minutes.

6 Meanwhile heat the butter in a small frying pan and add the chopped fresh coriander. Once this is frying, add it to the soup and stir in. Taste the soup and adjust accordingly.

7 Serve with crusty bread or toasted pitta.

TIP
• Half a chilli, chopped, can be added to the ingredients if a particularly warming soup is required.

Lentil and aubergine soup

When you expect more of a soup, this recipe has the answer. This soup will satisfy any soup cravings as it has lots of goodness as well as being comforting. Its consistency can be varied as required. It is good for eaters of all ages, especially children – I can't think of a better recipe to introduce lentils to children. This is a great soup, especially for winter days.

1 Thoroughly wash the lentils, then place them in a pot. Cover with 1.1 litres (2 pints) of the boiling water, bring back to the boil, then reduce heat to a gentle simmer.

2 Meanwhile, heat the olive oil in a frying pan. Then add the onion and sugar. When the onions are slightly browned, add the chopped aubergine.

3 Allow the aubergine to sweat with the onions and cook until the mixture is soft.

4 Add the aubergine and onions to the simmering lentils and then add the last 1.1 litres (2 pints) of water. Cover the pot and continue to simmer the ingredients on a moderate heat for 30–45 minutes, until the lentils are cooked to a soup-like consistency. Check the soup regularly.

5 Add the cinnamon, cumin, salt and white pepper, and simmer for a further 5 minutes.

6 Liquidise your soup in a food processor or through a mouli.

7 Serve with croutons and lemon wedges on the side.

TIPS

- The consistency of the soup can be adjusted to one's taste, so feel free to add more water if a thinner soup is required.
- 25 ml (1 fl oz) of freshly squeezed lemon juice can be added just before serving; this will help bring out the flavours.
- Any leftovers can be used as a base for a sauce to be served with pasta, or as a dip.
- Melba toast or toasted pitta bread can replace the croutons.
- The lemon wedges are for squeezing over the soup at the table if desired.

Shourbat adas ma' bitinjan

SERVES: **4**
PREPARATION TIME: **15 minutes**
COOKING TIME: **50–60 minutes**

225 g (8 oz) red lentils (split red lentils can be used, but small red lentils are preferable)

2.3 litres (4 pints) boiling water

110 ml (4 fl oz) extra virgin olive oil

1 onion, peeled and finely chopped

1 teaspoon granulated sugar

1 aubergine, peeled and chopped

½ teaspoon cinnamon

½ teaspoon cumin

1½ teaspoons salt

½ teaspoon white pepper

TO GARNISH
croutons, see p. 33

lemon wedges

Lentil and pimento soup

This is another soup that uses lentils. It is great during Ramadan as it is very substantial and provides energy food in its simplest form.

SERVES: **4**

PREPARATION TIME: **15 minutes**

COOKING TIME: **50–60 minutes**

225 g (8 oz) red lentils (split red lentils can be used, but small red lentils are preferable)

2.3 litres (4 pints) boiling water

110 ml (4 fl oz) extra virgin olive oil

1 onion, peeled and finely sliced

1 red pimento, deseeded and finely sliced

1 teaspoon granulated sugar

½ teaspoon cinnamon

½ teaspoon cumin

1½ teaspoons salt

½ teaspoon white pepper

TO GARNISH

croutons, see p. 33

lemon wedges

1   Thoroughly wash the lentils, then place them in a pot. Cover with 1.1 litres (2 pints) of the boiling water, bring back to the boil, then reduce heat to a gentle simmer.

2   Meanwhile, heat the olive oil in a frying pan. Then add the onion, pimento and sugar. Let the onions and pimento caramelise on a high heat, without burning.

3   Add the mixture in the frying pan to the simmering lentils. Cover the pot and continue to simmer gently for 25–30 minutes,

4   Add the cinnamon, cumin, salt and pepper, and simmer for a further 5 minutes.

5   Liquidise your soup in a food processor or through a mouli, and adjust the seasoning to taste.

6   Serve with croutons.

TIPS

- 25 ml (1 fl oz) of freshly squeezed lemon juice can be added to the soup before serving. Alternatively, lemon wedges can be placed on the table for individuals to squeeze over the soup to their own taste.

- This soup can be frozen once cooled, to be reheated when required.

Lentil and spinach soup

Here is another version of lentil soup. This one has a lighter and more summery feel to it than Lentil and aubergine *(see p. 53) and* Lentil and pimento *(see p. 54). It can be served as a light summer lunch accompanied by a salad and toasted pitta bread, or as a starter for a barbecue or summer dinner party. It is quick and easy to make, and does not have to be liquidised. A great asset to the soup collection.*

1 Heat the olive oil in a large pot. Then add the onion and sugar. Let the onions sauté on a high heat without browning them.

2 Add the spinach and mix together.

3 Thoroughly wash the lentils, then add to the onion and spinach mixture. Add 1.1 litres (2 pints) of the boiling water and bring back to the boil, then reduce the heat to a gentle simmer and leave for 10–15 minutes.

4 Pour in the rest of the water, bring to the boil then reduce heat to a gentle simmer for a further 15 minutes until the lentils are of a soup-like texture.

5 Add the cinnamon, cumin, salt and pepper, and simmer for a further 5 minutes.

6 Add the lemon juice, taste and adjust accordingly. Serve.

TIPS

• Check the soup constantly, ensuring that it does not overboil.

• Chard can be used instead of spinach if you like.

• Lemon juice can be omitted, and lemon wedges served at the table if preferred.

• The consistency of the soup can be varied, so liquidise it a little if you like.

Shourbat adas ma' sabanech

SERVES: **4**
PREPARATION TIME: **15 minutes**
COOKING TIME: **50 minutes**

75 ml (3 fl oz) extra virgin olive oil

1 onion, peeled and finely chopped

1 teaspoon granulated sugar

175 g (6 oz) fresh spinach, roughly chopped

175 g (6 oz) red lentils (split red lentils can be used, but small red lentils are preferable)

2.3 litres (4 pints) boiling water

½ teaspoon cinnamon

½ teaspoon cumin

1 teaspoon salt

½ teaspoon white pepper

25 ml (1 fl oz) lemon juice

Vegetable soup

SERVES: **4**

PREPARATION TIME: **15 minutes**

COOKING TIME: **30 minutes**

25 ml (1 fl oz) extra virgin olive oil

75 g (3 oz) unsalted butter

1 onion, peeled and chopped

1 teaspoon granulated sugar

2 carrots, peeled and finely sliced

2 medium-sized courgettes,
peeled and thinly sliced

110 g (4 oz) white button mushrooms,
thinly sliced

25 ml (1 fl oz) lemon juice

50 g (2 oz) chopped fresh parsley

½ teaspoon cinnamon

1 teaspoon ground cardamom

1½ teaspoons salt

½ teaspoon white pepper

1.75 litres (3 pints) boiling water

50 g (2 oz) vermicelli, broken
into pieces (see p. 28)

This soup is very popular during Ramadan, the fasting month, because it is nourishing without spoiling one's appetite for the second course. The soup can be prepared with any combination of vegetables; the list in this recipe is just a suggestion, so let your tastebuds guide you. I am sure the result will be just as good, if not better!

1 Heat the oil and 25 g (1 oz) of the butter in a large pot. Add the onion and sugar and cook until lightly browned.

2 Add the carrots and cook until they are light brown. Then add the courgettes, mushrooms, lemon juice and chopped parsley, stirring continuously.

3 Add the cinnamon, cardamom, salt and pepper, and continue to stir the mixture to make sure all the spices are fried to release their flavours.

4 Pour the water on to the mixture, bring back to the boil and then add the rest of the butter and vermicelli. Cover with a lid, then simmer on a moderate heat for 20 minutes.

5 Taste and adjust accordingly before serving. If it is Ramadan: *Siam makboul!* (May God accept you fasting!)

TIPS

• The way the vegetables are chopped will affect the whole look of the soup; the more finely they are chopped the better.

• Do not, however, be tempted to liquidise the soup, as this will spoil both its texture and look.

• 1 tablespoon of double cream may be added before serving if a creamier soup is preferred.

Chicken soup

This is the jewel of all soups. It is creamy as well as light, and is a great comfort to those with flu or cold symptoms.

TO PREPARE THE CHICKEN AND THE STOCK

1 In a large pot, heat the olive oil. Brown the chicken on all sides on a high heat. It should take about 5 minutes.

2 Pour the 2.3 litres (4 pints) of boiling water into the pot, then add the salt, cardamom pods, peppercorns, onion, lemon and carrot. Bring back to the boil, then reduce heat to a simmer. Cover and leave to simmer for 40–60 minutes.

3 Once the chicken is cooked, strain the stock into a large jug and put to one side. Take the chicken out of the pot and leave it on a plate or tray to cool. (While the chicken is cooling, you might like to wash out your pot because you'll need it to make the soup.)

4 When the chicken is cool enough, remove the meat from the bones and shred into small pieces.

TO MAKE THE SOUP

5 In your cleaned pot, heat the remaining olive oil. Add the onion and sugar and cook lightly. Then add the cardamom, pepper, cinnamon, chicken pieces and flour. Stir these ingredients together.

6 Add your chicken stock, vermicelli, butter, lemon juice and salt, and adjust seasoning to taste. Simmer for 10–15 minutes.

7 Mix the cornflour with cold water to form a paste, then add to the soup to thicken it. Serve.

TIPS

- The best way to remove the meat from the bone is either to wear cooking gloves, or to have a bowl of cold water by your side, and keep dipping in and cooling your hands.

- Do not be tempted to liquidise this soup, it will not do it any justice.

- 25 ml (1 fl oz) of double cream may be added towards the final stages of cooking if a creamier soup is preferred.

- This soup can be frozen once cooled, to be defrosted when needed.

Shourbat dajaj

SERVES: **6–8**

PREPARATION TIME: **20 minutes**

COOKING TIME: **1–1¼ hours**

FOR THE CHICKEN STOCK

50 ml (2 fl oz) extra virgin olive oil

1 chicken, cleaned, washed and dried

2.3 litres (4 pints) boiling water

1 teaspoon salt

5 whole cardamom pods

4 black peppercorns

½ onion, peeled

½ lemon

1 carrot

TO COMPLETE THE SOUP

25 ml (1 fl oz) extra virgin olive oil

1 medium onion, very finely chopped

1 teaspoon granulated sugar

1 teaspoon ground cardamom

½ teaspoon white pepper

½ teaspoon cinnamon

the prepared chicken pieces

1 tablespoon plain flour

the prepared chicken stock

50 g (2 oz) vermicelli, broken into pieces (see p. 28)

50 g (2 oz) unsalted butter

1 tablespoon lemon juice

1½ teaspoons salt

25 g (1 oz) cornflour

25 ml (1 fl oz) cold water

Meatball soup

When I want to give my children a treat, I make this soup for them. It is a great snack, starter or light lunch. See the opposite page for the finished result.

SERVES: **4**

PREPARATION TIME: **20 minutes**

COOKING TIME: **30–35 minutes**

FOR THE MEATBALLS

225 g (8 oz) minced lamb

¼ onion, peeled and finely chopped

¼ red pepper, deseeded and very finely chopped (optional)

1 clove garlic, peeled and finely chopped

¼ teaspoon cinnamon

½ teaspoon salt

¼ teaspoon white pepper

110 ml (4 fl oz) extra virgin olive oil

FOR THE SOUP

50 ml (2 fl oz) extra virgin olive oil

25 g (1 oz) unsalted butter

½ medium onion, peeled and finely sliced

1 teaspoon granulated sugar

1 teaspoon ground cardamom

1½ teaspoons salt

¼ teaspoon white pepper

½ teaspoon cinnamon

1 tablespoon chopped fresh parsley

the prepared meatballs

1.75 litres (3 pints) boiling water

50 g (2 oz) unsalted butter

50 g (2 oz) vermicelli, broken into pieces (see p. 28)

2 carrots, peeled and cut into chunks

TO PREPARE THE MEATBALLS

1 Place the minced lamb, onion, pepper (if using), garlic, cinnamon, salt, pepper and half the olive oil in the food processor and pulse the ingredients together once or twice.

2 Tip out the mixture and form into small balls. (You should be able to make about 30 very small ones.)

3 In a frying pan, heat the rest of the olive oil. Then gently fry the meatballs for about 4 minutes, moving them around in the pan to make sure they all become brown.

TO MAKE THE SOUP

4 In a pot, heat the olive oil and butter. Then add the onion and sugar until they are light brown.

5 Add the cardamom, salt, pepper, cinnamon, parsley and the fried meatballs and mix together.

6 Pour in the boiling water. Add the butter, vermicelli and carrots, bring back to the boil and then gently simmer the mixture for 20 minutes until the liquid thickens slightly.

7 Taste and adjust accordingly, then serve in large bowls!

TIPS

- When making the meatballs, wet the palm of your hand with water as this will make the job easier.
- The meatballs can be made any size, but the smaller they are the better.

Shourbat banadoura

SERVES: **4**

PREPARATION TIME: **20 minutes**

COOKING TIME: **30 minutes**

50 ml (2 fl oz) extra virgin olive oil

1 small onion, peeled
and finely chopped

1 teaspoon granulated sugar

4 beef tomatoes or 6 salad tomatoes,
skinned and finely chopped

½ teaspoon cinnamon

½ teaspoon ground allspice

1½ teaspoons salt

½ teaspoon white pepper

50 g (2 oz) unsalted butter

1.4 litres (2½ pints) boiling water

225 g (8 oz) tin chopped tomatoes,
sieved

50 g (2 oz) vermicelli, broken
into pieces (see p. 28)

TO GARNISH
1 tablespoon chopped fresh mint

Tomato soup

This creamy, smooth and full-bodied soup is ideal to make during the summer months, when tomatoes are at their best, being abundant and at the peak of their flavour. It's also a firm favourite with children of any age.

1   In a pot, heat the olive oil. Add the onion and sugar and fry until light brown.

2   Add the fresh tomatoes, cinnamon, allspice, salt and pepper.

3   Mix the spices with the tomatoes and onion and cook on a moderate heat for 5 minutes, stirring occasionally.

4   Add the butter, then the boiling water. Add the sieved tinned tomatoes and vermicelli and simmer gently on a medium to low heat for 20 minutes until thickened.

5   Adjust to taste and serve in warmed bowls with chopped mint.

TIPS

•   To skin your tomatoes, cut a cross in the bottom with a sharp knife. Then plunge into boiling water for 1 minute. The skin should come away easily when peeled.

•   Beef tomatoes are best for this recipe, as they are fleshier and there is no need to deseed them.

•   The soup is thick enough to be served as a main course, accompanied by a green salad and toasted pitta bread.

•   If you would like to liquidise your soup, omit the vermicelli as otherwise it will be too thick.

Spinach and rocket soup

Spinach is probably the most underrated vegetable. It is so versatile, and it is very easy to make a spinach dish quickly. We just have to put some thought into the combinations that will best complement its natural flavours. This soup, I am sure, will give children in particular the right idea about spinach. It is very simple and good fast food at its best.

1 Heat half the olive oil, butter, onion and sugar in a medium-sized pot and sauté together until translucent.

2 Add the spinach, salt, white pepper and ground coriander and mix together.

3 Add the stock, lower the heat to medium, and allow the soup to simmer for 2 minutes.

4 Add the rocket leaves and simmer for 2 more minutes.

5 Meanwhile, heat the rest of the olive oil in a small frying pan, add the finely chopped garlic and sauté for a few seconds, then add the chopped coriander leaves and mix and fry together for a few seconds. (Alternatively, if you have some *Coriander and garlic paste* (p. 36) already made you could instead add a couple of tablespoons to your taste to the mixture at this stage.)

6 Pour the garlic and coriander mixture into the soup and switch off the heat.

7 Put half of the soup in a blender or food processor and liquidise. Add the liquidised soup to the other half and mix together.

8 Serve the soup topped with fresh rocket leaves and croutons or toasted pitta bread.

TIPS

• Rocket can be replaced with the same amount of spinach if preferred.

• The soup can be cooked with plain boiling water rather than stock if preferred – this will mean the soup is lighter but just as tasty.

• Frozen spinach can be used, without needing to be defrosted. Add it frozen, after the onions, add the water and follow the recipe allowing 2 more minutes for cooking the spinach.

Shourbat sabanech ma' rocca

SERVES: **4**
PREPARATION TIME: **15 minutes**
COOKING TIME: **20 minutes**

50 ml (2 fl oz) extra virgin olive oil

50 g (2 oz) butter

1 medium onion, peeled and finely chopped

1 teaspoon granulated sugar

225 g (8 oz) fresh spinach, roughly chopped

1 teaspoon salt

½ teaspoon white pepper

1 teaspoon ground coriander

1.4 litres (2½ pints) chicken or vegetable stock

100 g (4 oz) rocket leaves

3 cloves garlic, peeled and very finely chopped

25 g (1 oz) fresh coriander, finely chopped

TO SERVE
50 g (2 oz) rocket leaves

croutons (see p. 33) or toasted pitta bread

Pumpkin soup

Pumpkin is an unappreciated vegetable. Yet it is a package of flavour, vitamins, minerals, colour and above all creaminess of taste and texture. There is also an overwhelming feeling of satisfaction once it is eaten, whether in soup form, as a casserole or as a side dish. Peeling and preparing pumpkin is not pleasurable but it is a job worth doing. This soup can be a starter to a light main course, or a main course served with a salad. It is popular with all ages, even babies. Any kind of pumpkin will do as long as it is fresh.

SERVES: 4
PREPARATION TIME: 20 minutes
COOKING TIME: 25 minutes

75 ml (3 fl oz) extra virgin olive oil

1 onion, peeled and finely chopped

1 teaspoon granulated sugar

700 g (1½ lb) pumpkin, peeled and diced

2 cm (¾ inch) root ginger, peeled and chopped

2 carrots, peeled and sliced

1 potato, peeled and chopped

1 teaspoon salt

½ teaspoon white pepper

½ teaspoon ground coriander

2 litres (3½ pints) boiling water

50 g (2 oz) butter

1 tablespoon lemon juice

75 ml (3 fl oz) double cream

TO SERVE
toasted pitta bread

salad of rocket leaves

1 Heat a large heavy pan, add the olive oil, onion and sugar and sauté on a high heat for a minute.

2 Add the pumpkin and mix together.

3 Add the chopped root ginger, carrots, potato, salt, white pepper and coriander and mix together for a minute or so.

4 Pour in the boiling water, add the butter and cover with lid. Allow to simmer gently on a moderate heat for 20 minutes.

5 Liquidise the soup and then pour back into the pan. Add the lemon juice and the cream and serve when you are ready.

TIPS

• The cream can be omitted and served on the side instead if you prefer.

• The consistency of the soup can be determined through personal preference. Feel free to thin the soup by adding more water.

• Rocket leaves give a nice contrast with their fresh, peppery taste.

Get better soup

This soup is the key to recovery from illness. It is my grandmother's recipe, and it's an instant remedy! It worked for her and it works for me. I hope it works for you too.

1 Heat a large deep pot and add the oil, followed by the lamb pieces. Turn the meat on all sides to brown it.

2 Add the onion to the pot, and fry with the meat. Add the *freekeh* and mix in.

3 Add the cinnamon, cardamom, saffron, cumin, salt and pepper, then the boiling water. Cover the pot with a lid, lower the heat and allow the contents to simmer for 50 minutes, checking the soup throughout the cooking.

4 Add the lemon juice and seasoning to taste, and check the meat is tender and well cooked, then serve. Good health always!

TIPS

• Any other lamb joint could be used, not necessarily a cutlet, as long as the meat is on the bone.

• Lemon wedges can be served on the side. Lemon juice enhances the flavour wonderfully and it all adds to the recovery process.

• If *freekeh* is not available, replace with 50 g (2 oz) pudding rice. Wash the rice and add it 30 minutes after the meat is added. Cook for a further 20 minutes. Just as effective and healthy.

SERVES: **4**

PREPARATION TIME: **15 minutes**

COOKING TIME: **60 minutes**

75 ml (3 fl oz) olive oil

700 g (1 lb 8 oz) lamb cutlets, with fat removed

1 medium onion, peeled and finely chopped

110 g (4 oz) *freekeh* (see p. 24), washed twice and soaked in 570 ml (1 pint) of lukewarm water for 10 minutes

½ teaspoon cinnamon

1 teaspoon ground cardamom

½ teaspoon saffron

½ teaspoon cumin

1½ teaspoons salt

1 teaspoon white pepper

2.3 litres (4 pints) boiling water

50 ml (2 fl oz) lemon juice

TO SERVE
lemon wedges

MEZZE: STARTERS AND SAVOURY SNACKS

Here is where Lebanese cuisine comes into its own. There is such a rich feast of ingredients that can be combined to make mouth-watering starters or *mezze* items, snacks and even picnics. And the best part? Because most of these foods are served cold, they can be prepared well in advance of meal times, leaving you, the cook, time to relax and enjoy the food.

Perfect hommous

Hommous is the most popular of all mezze dishes. It is a dip made with a blend of chickpeas and tahini paste. Full of protein, it is energy food at its best. It is very simple to make once one has mastered the technique. Tinned chickpeas can be used but they won't give the smooth texture of soaked and boiled ones. If these instructions are followed, success is guaranteed.

SERVES: **at least 4–6**

PREPARATION TIME: **20 minutes (plus overnight soaking time)**

COOKING TIME: **20 minutes**

350 g (12 oz) chickpeas, soaked overnight in double their quantity of cold water

2.3 litres (4 pints) cold water

25 g (1 oz) bicarbonate of soda

175 ml (6 fl oz) tahini

4 or 5 ice cubes

1 tablespoon salt

225 ml (8 fl oz) lemon juice

TO GARNISH

2 tablespoons of whole cooked chickpeas

1 tablespoon chopped fresh parsley

¼ teaspoon paprika

drizzle of olive oil

1 Strain the chickpeas that have been soaking overnight, then rinse under cold running water. Prepare as per the method on p. 49, using the quantities listed here.

2 Drain the peas thoroughly and leave in a colander.

3 Reserve about 2 tablespoons of the cooked chickpeas for the garnish.

4 Place the chickpeas in a food processor and process until you have a fine mixture.

5 Add the tahini and the ice cubes and process again until smooth. Add the salt and lemon juice. Process briefly to incorporate these ingredients. Taste the mixture and adjust the seasoning and amount of lemon juice to your taste. Allow the hommous to chill for a few minutes before serving.

6 Serve in a shallow dish, with whole chickpeas in the middle (optional). Use parsley and a sprinkle of paprika to garnish, and drizzle with a little olive oil if required. Refer to the picture opposite for the finished result.

TIPS

• Take care that the chickpeas are perfectly cooked before taking them off the heat and rinsing them as this will affect the final result.

• Ice cubes are used in the preparation of the hommous rather than water as they help retain its texture. You can add 50 ml (2 fl oz) cold water at this point if the mixture is too thick, but ensure that it doesn't become too runny.

• The hommous can be stored covered with clingfilm in the coldest part of the refrigerator for up to a week.

• Always mix the hommous well before serving it to loosen it and provide the rich gloss on its surface.

Hommous kawerma

SERVES: **4**

PREPARATION TIME: **for the Hommous: 20 minutes (plus overnight soaking time) for the meat: 20 minutes**

COOKING TIME: **5 minutes**

FOR THE HOMMOUS
see p. 66

FOR THE MEAT
2 tablespoons olive oil or ghee

225 g (8 oz) shoulder of lamb, diced

½ teaspoon salt

½ teaspoon white pepper

TO GARNISH
25 g (1 oz) pine nuts, sautéed in a little olive oil

TO ACCOMPANY
Fattoush (see p. 69) and pickles (see pp. 40–4)

Hommous with lamb

This is the connoisseur's version of hommous; the combination of hommous and lamb is one made in heaven. The meat should be lean – shoulder of lamb is best, as it is sweet and tender enough to flash fry.

1 In a heavy frying pan, heat the olive oil or ghee. Add the meat and sauté on a high heat, shaking the pan rather than stirring.

2 Allow to fry for a minute or so, adding the salt and pepper, so that the meat is browned evenly without overcooking.

3 Put the hommous into a serving dish, and create a central cavity into which you can place the cooked meat.

4 Garnish with lightly sautéed pine nuts and drizzle with the oil in which the meat has been fried.

TIPS

• Ghee is best for frying the meat as it withstands the high temperature well. It also has a better flavour than oil.

• The meat must be fried on a high heat, so it is cooked as quickly as possible. Do not overcook however, otherwise it will become too dry.

• The meat used should be free from fat and diced evenly so that it cooks evenly.

• The dish should be served instantly to be enjoyed to the full.

Fattoush

Fattoush is the most important salad in Lebanese cuisine. The texture varies according to how you choose to chop the vegetables, but one should aim for a chunky effect. The dressing will remain the same, with sumac as its main ingredient. Pomegranate seeds contribute to the contrast of textures and add sweetness.

1 Place the tomatoes, cucumber, lettuce, radishes, peppers, parsley and mint in a bowl.

2 In a screw-top jar, mix the sumac, dried mint, sugar, salt, vinegar, lemon juice and olive oil. Then pour over and toss the salad.

3 Scatter on the croutons and pomegranate seeds and serve.

TIPS

- The fresher your salad ingredients, the better your salad will taste.

- Rocket leaves (when in season) are a great ingredient for this salad.

- The salad can be prepared will in advance, kept in the refrigerator covered with cling film and dressed just before serving.

- Pitta bread cut into small squares and toasted under the grill until light brown can be used as an alternative to croutons.

SERVES: 4

PREPARATION TIME: 15 minutes

2 beef tomatoes or 4 salad tomatoes, coarsely chopped

2 small cucumbers, peeled and sliced

1 Cos lettuce, roughly chopped

1 bunch radishes (about 10), halved

1 green pepper, deseeded and roughly chopped

1 red pepper, deseeded and roughly chopped

75 g (3 oz) flat leaf parsley, roughly chopped

50 g (2 oz) fresh mint leaves, roughly chopped

3 spring onions, roughly chopped

FOR THE DRESSING
2 teaspoons sumac (see p. 27)

1 teaspoon dried mint

½ teaspoon granulated sugar

2 teaspoons salt

25 ml (1 fl oz) red wine vinegar

75 ml (3 fl oz) lemon juice

110 ml (4 fl oz) extra virgin olive oil

TO GARNISH
2 tablespoons croutons (see p. 33)

75 g (3 oz) pomegranate seeds

Tabbouleh

SERVES: **4**

PREPARATION TIME: **20 minutes**

COOKING TIME: **5 minutes**

3 bunches flat leaf parsley

50 g (2 oz) fresh mint leaves

1 heaped tablespoon brown burgul
(or, alternatively, fine white)

6 salad tomatoes or 2 beef
tomatoes, finely chopped

Parsley is the main ingredient in Tabbouleh and the way it is chopped is the key to the texture, taste and overall presentation of the salad. It is the most popular Lebanese salad. A sharp knife is essential to shred, rather than chop, the parsley. This also applies to the mint leaves. The tomatoes must be firm. Beef tomatoes can also be used. Removing the seeds is not necessary as they aren't really noticeable in the salad, and the juice in the tomatoes provides sufficient liquid for soaking the burgul. The burgul can be white or brown depending on what is available, although I prefer the brown as it has a more nutty flavour and retains its crunch.

1　Take the bunch of parsley, twist it around once or twice and chop off the stalks with a knife. Start to chop using a shredding action, by

twisting the parsley while chopping finely, making sure not to go over any bits twice.

2 Chop the mint leaves in the same way and mix with the parsley.

3 Add the burgul. Place the chopped tomatoes on top of the burgul.

4 Leave in the refrigerator until needed, by which time the burgul should have softened from the juice of the tomatoes.

TO PREPARE THE DRESSING

5 Prepare the dressing by mixing together the chopped spring onions, salt, sumac, olive oil, lemon juice and dried mint in a jar, putting on the lid and shaking it vigourously. Leave to one side until you are ready to serve.

TO SERVE

6 Place the mixture in a dish or on a platter, pour the dressing over it and mix in and arrange lettuce leaves around it. Place the chopped tomatoes on top. Enjoy!

TIPS

- *Tabbouleh* can be prepared in advance, but don't add the dressing until just before you are ready to serve.

- The burgul does not need to be soaked in water. You will get a tastier result if it is arranged in layers with the chopped tomatoes. It softens while waiting to be dressed and served. If, however, you wish to serve the *Tabbouleh* instantly, soak the burgul with just enough water to cover it while you are chopping the salad ingredients.

- Always taste and adjust the *Tabbouleh* before serving, with salt, lemon juice or olive oil as necessary.

- Don't leave it to stand to long as it will become too soggy.

FOR THE DRESSING

6 spring onions, washed and chopped

1 teaspoon salt

1 tablespoon sumac (see p. 27)

110 ml (4 fl oz) extra virgin olive oil

75 ml (3 fl oz) lemon juice

1 teaspoon dried mint (optional)

TO GARNISH

1 Cos or little gem lettuce

1 tablespoon chopped salad tomatoes

Salata zeitoun

SERVES: **4**

PREPARATION TIME: **20 minutes**

3 beef tomatoes or 6 salad tomatoes

3 spring onions, finely chopped

1 tablespoon chopped flat leaf parsley

1 tablespoon chopped fresh mint

75 g (3 oz) black or green olives,
pitted and halved

1 teaspoon salt

3 tablepoons extra virgin olive oil

TO GARNISH
¼ teaspoon sumac (see p. 27)

fresh mint or fresh parsley sprigs

lemon slices or wedges

Olive salad

This is the best self-dressed salad I know. It was created for one of my favourite clients Sheikh Mohammed Bin Rashid al-Maktoum who would insist on this dish to accompany his meal. The combination of the oil and the tomatoes, together with the salt, produces a wonderful dressing which gives it its distinctive, mild flavour.

1 Slice tomatoes widthways into thick slices, then halve each slice. Chop these pieces into small rectangles.

2 Put the tomatoes in a bowl. Add the spring onions, parsley, mint, olives, salt and olive oil, and mix gently.

3 To serve, put the salad on a flat dish and sprinkle on the sumac. Garnish with mint or parsley sprigs and slices or wedges of lemon.

TIPS

* Beef tomatoes are best for this recipe, but as long as they are firm you can use other varieties too.

* Do not skin or deseed the tomatoes, as these parts are vital to the texture of the salad.

* Do not be tempted to add lemon juice to the salad, as the sumac will provide the sour flavour needed.

* This salad is a great accompaniment to any meal, particularly rice dishes.

SERVES: **2–4**

PREPARATION TIME: **15 minutes**

1 Cos lettuce, washed thoroughly

1 bunch parsley (preferably flat leaf)

FOR THE DRESSING
2 tablespoons chopped spring onions

1 tablespoon sumac (see p. 27)

Lebanese caesar salad

This salad is the simplest salad you can imagine. I discovered it by accident when having to create a salad with just a few ingredients and since then this salad has become a family favourite. It is very versatile as an accompaniment, but is especially suited to rich dishes as it provides a contrast to cleanse the palate. It is full of vitamins and minerals especially if it is served soon after it is prepared without chilling; it tastes best at room temperature.

1 Mix the dressing ingredients in a glass jar with a lid, shake the jar well and keep in the refrigerator until ready to use.

2 Chop the Cos lettuce roughly. Chop the parsley finely and mix into the lettuce.

3 Dress the salad by tossing with the dressing. Serve immediately.

TIPS

- Iceberg lettuce or any other chunky lettuce can be used, but Cos lettuce is best because of its strong distinctive taste.

- The salad dressing can be prepared well in advance and kept in the refrigerator.

- The salad can be enhanced by using more than one kind of lettuce e.g. rocket, lamb's lettuce, endive etc.

- Croutons can be thrown into the salad, but I prefer it without.

1 teaspoon salt

½ teaspoon freshly ground black pepper

75 ml (3 fl oz) extra virgin olive oil

50 ml (2 fl oz) lemon juice

½ teaspoon Dijon mustard

½ teaspoon granulated sugar, or honey

Tahini salad

This salad is a combination of flavour, comfort and satisfaction, and is an exotic as well nutritious accompaniment to any dish, whether it involves chicken, lamb, beef, fish, eggs or a vegetarian dish as it is so versatile and improves in flavour if it is kept in the refrigerator (for up to a week, chilled and covered). I had to include it for these reasons especially as life is getting busier, and good leftovers are very much appreciated.

1 Mix the tahini with the salt and water very well to form a sauce. Add the lemon juice, mix in and set aside.

2 In another bowl mix the tomatoes, cucumber, radishes, peppers, garlic, spring onions, Cos lettuce and parsley. Add the tahini dressing, taste, adjust and serve.

TIPS

- The tomatoes can be peeled if they are firm; the result will be a smoother, silkier salad.

- Beef tomatoes can be used to get a chunkier salad, but reduce the amount of tomatoes proportionally.

Salata bi tahini

SERVES: 4

PREPARATION TIME: 15 minutes

FOR THE TAHINI DRESSING
110 ml (4 fl oz) tahini

1 tablespoon salt

110 ml (4 fl oz) water

150 ml (5 fl oz) lemon juice

FOR THE SALAD
4 medium salad tomatoes, finely chopped

1 small cucumber or ¼ large cucumber, peeled and finely chopped

4 radishes, finely chopped

½ sweet red pepper, deseeded and finely chopped

½ green pepper, deseeded and finely chopped

1 clove garlic, peeled and finely
chopped

1 spring onion, finely chopped

½ Cos lettuce, finely chopped

½ bunch flat leaf parsley, finely
chopped

- The fresher the salad ingredients the better the salad and the longer its life.
- A sharp knife will help you avoid any bruising of the vegetables.
- Feel free to add more or less lemon juice according to your taste, but remember the result should not be overpowering.
- The flavour of the salad matures in the refrigerator.

Moutabbal

SERVES: **4**
PREPARATION TIME: **15 minutes**
COOKING TIME: **15 minutes**

2 aubergines, washed and left whole
1 teaspoon salt
125 ml (4 fl oz) tahini
125 ml (4 fl oz) lemon juice

TO GARNISH
1 tablespoon chopped fresh parsley
1 tablespoon pomegranate seeds
fresh mint leaves

Aubergine dip

The caviar of Lebanese mezze, this is a light yet highly flavoured salad. The quality of the aubergines is vital, as their bitterness and amount of grilling determines the overall result.

1 Slash the flesh of the aubergines with the point of a sharp knife.

2 Place the aubergines on an open flame each. Chargrill until the skins blister, being careful not to overcook them.

3 Put the grilled aubergines on a baking tray to catch the juices.

4 While the aubergines are still warm, peel off their skins under cold running water and allow them to cool on a tray.

5 Tip the aubergine juices from the tray into a jug and reserve.

6 Place the skinned aubergines into a food processor and pulse quickly once or twice – don't overdo it.

7 Scoop out the pulped aubergine flesh and transfer it to a bowl. Add the reserved juices, salt, tahini and lemon juice, and mix well.

8 Taste and adjust seasoning accordingly, then place in an airtight container and chill for 1 hour in the refrigerator. This will firm it up.

9 To serve, garnish with fresh parsley, pomegranate seeds and fresh mint leaves.

TIPS
- Chargrilling the aubergines on an open flame is vital as it creates the smoky flavour which makes this dish distinctive.

- The aubergines can be kept in the refrigerator after being grilled, peeled and cooled to be used when required.

- The pomegranates seeds add texture and contrast to the dip.

- To make the dip chunkier, you can mash the chargrilled aubergines instead of processing them.

- It is better to use less tahini, as more of the flavour of the aubergines will come out.

Chargrilled aubergine salad

Beitinjan el raheb

This is another way of using chargrilled aubergines. It is a light salad and of less calorific value than Aubergine dip as no tahini is used. It is very popular when accompanied by other Lebanese mezze dishes, or on its own as part of a meal accompanying a roast or vegetarian equivalent.

SERVES: **4**

PREPARATION TIME: **20 minutes**

COOKING TIME: **15 minutes**

1 Follow the preparation of the aubergines as for the *Aubergine dip* recipe (p. 74) up to and including stage 5.

2 Chop the aubergines finely, and then transfer to a bowl. Add the reserved juices, salt, tomatoes, radishes, spring onions, parsley, garlic, pomegranate syrup, lemon juice and olive oil and mix together lightly without damaging the ingredients. Taste and adjust seasoning accordingly.

3 Transfer to a flat dish, sprinkle with pine nuts and pomegranate seeds, and serve.

2 aubergines, washed and left whole

1 teaspoon salt

1 beef tomato or 3 salad tomatoes, finely chopped

5 small radishes, finely chopped

3 spring onions, finely chopped

2 tablespoons chopped fresh parsley

½ teaspoon garlic, finely chopped

½ tablespoon pomegranate syrup (see p. 26)

50 ml (2 fl oz) lemon juice

25 ml (1 fl oz) extra virgin olive oil

TIPS

- A sharp knife is vital for chopping the tomatoes and the rest of the ingredients, to prevent bruising of the ingredients.

- Chopping the aubergines rather than processing them gives texture to the salad, thus differentiating it from a dip.

- To maximise the flavour, add in half a clove of garlic, finely chopped.

TO GARNISH

lightly sautéed pine nuts (see p. 26)

1 tablespoon pomegranate seeds

Yoghurt cheese

Home-made cheese made from yoghurt is a must in almost all Lebanese households. It is eaten at breakfast, for snacks and as a light meal. It is full of goodness and has great versatility, which makes it one of the most essential basic dishes on the Lebanese table.

SERVES: **4 (this recipe will yield about 275 g (10 oz) of *labneh*)**

PREPARATION TIME: **overnight, plus 4–6 hours thereafter**

900 ml (1½ pints) *Home-made yoghurt* (see p. 34) or other plain yoghurt

½ teaspoon salt

TO GARNISH

½ teaspoon dried mint

a few fresh mint leaves

50 g (2 oz) black olives, pitted

extra virgin olive oil

YOU WILL ALSO NEED

a muslin bag

a side plate and heavy object such as a can of tomatoes

an airtight container

1 Mix the yoghurt and salt together, and place in the muslin bag to strain. Hang the bag in a cool, clean place overnight, with a bowl underneath to catch the liquid.

2 Put the bag in a colander balanced over a bowl; put the plate and heavy object on top of the bag to squeeze out any remaining liquid.

3 Leave for a further 4–6 hours.

4 Remove the mixture from the bag and stir gently. Transfer to the airtight container and leave to chill in the refrigerator until ready to serve.

5 To serve, place on a flat plate and scatter with dried mint. Decorate with fresh mint leaves and olives, and drizzle with a little olive oil.

TIPS

- Making small batches ensures a creamier tasting *labneh*, as does using a creamy yoghurt.

- I recommend using *Home-made yoghurt* as I prefer the taste but any good quality shop-bought variety will do just as well.

- If a thinner consistency is required, omit the extra straining with the heavy weight.

- It is important that the yoghurt used is not too runny.

Yoghurt cheese balls

This a preserved version of labneh. *Sometimes one goes through all the trouble of preparing something, but is then unable to consume it when it is at its best. This method of preserving* labneh *enables one to relax about having to consume it by a certain date; it prolongs its shelf life by at least a month, especially if it is kept in the coldest part of the refrigerator. You can also be safe in the knowledge that the* labneh *will retain its creaminess and full flavour without being spoilt by the time factor.*

MAKES: **10 fl oz (½ pint) jar of labneh balls**

PREPARATION TIME: **overnight, plus 4–6 hours thereafter**

1 quantity of *Yoghurt cheese* (see p. 76)

YOU WILL ALSO NEED
a tray, covered with a clean tea towel or absorbent kitchen paper

a glass jar with an airtight lid, half-filled with 150 ml (6 fl oz) extra virgin olive oil

1   Follow the *Yoghurt cheese* recipe (p. 76) up to and including stage 3.

2   Remove from the muslin bag and place in a bowl. Form small balls of 1½ cm (¾ inch) in diameter.

3   Lay the balls on the tray covered with the kitchen cloth, and place in the refrigerator overnight to dry.

4   Take the tray out of the refrigerator and fill half the glass jar with 150 ml (6 fl oz) extra virgin olive oil.

5   Grease the palms of your hands with a bit of olive oil, and reshape the balls to make them smoother.

6   Drop the balls in the jar of oil gently and carefully, put on the lid of the jar and seal tightly. Place in the refrigerator until needed.

TIPS
• Use only extra virgin olive oil, because any other kind of olive oil will spoil the taste of the finished product.

• The overnight resting period is vital to their success as it guarantees that the balls are free of liquid and are completely dry.

• The jar should be tightly sealed.

• When taking the *Yoghurt cheese balls* out of the jar make sure that the utensil used is very clean, and the jar tightly resealed.

Shankleesh

MAKES: **4 balls, any extra of which can be frozen until required. A salad using 2 balls serves 4.**

PREPARATION TIME: **20 minutes**

COOKING TIME: **overnight plus 2 more hours for chilling**

FOR THE SHANKLEESH BALLS

225 g (8 oz) *Yoghurt cheese* (see p. 76)

110 g (4 oz) feta cheese

⅓ teaspoon chilli powder

½ teaspoon thyme

½ teaspoon cumin

½ teaspoon granulated sugar

½ teaspoon salt

½ teaspoon white pepper

FOR COATING THE SHANKLEESH BALLS

50 g (2 oz) thyme

FOR THE SALAD

1 beef tomato, chopped

1 medium red onion, peeled and finely sliced

1 tablespoon chopped fresh parsley

2 prepared Shankleesh balls

50 ml (2 fl oz) extra virgin olive oil

TO GARNISH

sprigs of flat leaf parsley

tomato slices

YOU WILL ALSO NEED

a tray, covered with a clean tea towel or absorbent kitchen paper

Yoghurt cheese salad

Shankleesh *(see picture opposite) represents the full richness of a true Lebanese salad. It is distinctly Lebanese because it is essential for mezze and complements Arab and Lebanese wines. It looks complicated to make but the recipe is easy to follow. Shankleesh balls can be bought from Lebanese delicatessens and specialist shops, ready to add to a salad, but the home-made version is always more special. I have tried to keep the ingredients simple and easy to get hold of.*

TO PREPARE THE SHANKLEESH BALLS

1 Mix together the yoghurt cheese, feta cheese, chilli powder, thyme, cumin, sugar, salt and pepper.

2 Cover a shallow tray with one of the clean tea towels which will absorb the juices, then place handfuls of the yoghurt cheese mixture on the tray.

3 Allow the mixture to dry overnight in the refrigerator.

4 Take the mixture from the refrigerator and form into balls (about 4). Roll the balls lightly in the extra thyme to coat.

5 Arrange the coated balls on a new tray on a new tea towel, cover in cling film and chill in the coolest part of the refrigerator for a minimum of 2 hours.

TO PREPARE THE SALAD

6 In a bowl, mix together the tomato, onion and parsley.

7 Break the *Shankleesh* balls into chunks and add to the salad mixture.

8 Carefully toss the salad in olive oil without breaking the *Shankleesh* pieces.

9 Garnish with flat leaf parsley and tomato slices and serve.

TIPS
- Toss the salad gently with your fingertips to ensure the cheese does not crumble.
- *Shankleesh* balls can be prepared well in advance – you can put them in freezer bags in the freezer and defrost them when required.
- You can use bought yoghurt cheese (*Labneh*) instead of making your own if you prefer.
- Spring onions can be used instead of the normal onion – just as delicious.

Mouhamara

SERVES: **4**

PREPARATION TIME: **20 minutes**

COOKING TIME: **15 minutes**

300 ml (½ pint) vegetable oil
for deep frying

50 g (2 oz) whole walnuts, shelled

75 g (3 oz) whole cashews, shelled

75 g (3 oz) blanched almonds

½ red pepper, deseeded
and finely chopped

½ onion, peeled and chopped

½ teaspoon salt

50 g (2 oz) *Red chilli sauce*
(see pp. 38–9)

110 ml (6 fl oz) extra virgin olive oil

TO GARNISH
a handful of pine nuts

slices of red pepper

YOU WILL ALSO NEED
a deep-fat fryer or deep frying pan

Nut salad

This is a great accompaniment to raw meat dishes, as its chunky nutty flavour contrasts with the mellow fine texture of the meat. It is a rich and exotic favourite.

1 In a deep-fat fryer, heat the vegetable oil to 425°F (220°C), or heat a little oil in a deep frying pan and fry separately the walnuts, cashews and almonds until they turn a rich, honey colour. It is important to fry each kind separately as they cook at different speeds.

2 Drain on absorbent kitchen paper and allow to dry.

3 When the nuts are cool, coarsely chop them in a food processor. Then place them in a bowl.

4 Into the bowl, add the pepper, onion, salt, chilli sauce and olive oil. Mix thoroughly.

5 To serve, arrange the mixture on a shallow or flat dish, then decorate with pine nuts and red pepper rings.

TIPS

*   The temperature of the oil should be high as the nuts have to be fried in just a few seconds so that they are coloured rather than cooked.

*   The consistency of this salad is determined by the amount of oil used; feel free to adjust to taste.

*   The salt is optional – add it according to your taste.

*   The nuts can be prepared in advance and stored in a jar in the refrigerator until needed.

Bean salad

In Lebanon, foul (a small kidney-shaped bean) is the main diet of people who don't have much money because it is cheap, readily available, rich in protein and very nourishing. Having said that, it is also served as a breakfast dish in many Lebanese homes and all over the Middle East; it is said that foul is the rich man's breakfast and the poor man's dinner. It is, however, healthy and delicious for everyone. My version requires Hommous balila (cooked chickpeas) to be mixed with the foul, which gives it a creamier taste and a good contrast in colour.

1 Rinse the soaked *foul* beans and place in a pan. Add the water and cover the pan with a lid. Bring to the boil, then simmer for 60 minutes until almost all of the water has been absorbed and the beans are cooked. Check the beans regularly during the 60 minutes, and add a drop more boiling water if you feel there isn't enough liquid in the pan.

2 Meanwhile rinse the soaked chickpeas, place in a pan and add 570 ml (1 pint) of water and bicarbonate of soda. Allow to come to the boil, then lower the heat to simmer the chickpeas for 10–15 minutes. Check the chickpeas: if their skins come off easily, they are ready. Rinse them under cold water and set aside to drain in a colander.

3 Place the hot cooked *foul* in a bowl and add half the chickpeas. Mash gently with the back of a spoon to a medium texture so that they are not too mushy.

4 Add the garlic, salt, lemon juice and olive oil.

5 Transfer the mixture to a large bowl and serve with the rest of the chickpeas and chopped parsley on top. Drizzle with the olive oil and accompany with tomatoes and green olives.

TIPS

• The quality and freshness of the beans will affect the final result, so always check the sell-by date.

• Make sure you check the beans throughout their cooking and keep them covered with a lid to help tenderise them.

• Once cooked, the beans can be reserved and used at a later date if necessary.

Foul medamas

SERVES: **4**
PREPARATION TIME: **15 minutes**
COOKING TIME: **60–70 minutes**

225 g (8 oz) dry *foul*, soaked overnight in double their quantity of water

1.1 litres (2 pints) cold water

2 cloves garlic, peeled and very finely chopped

2 teaspoons salt

75 ml (3 fl oz) lemon juice

50 ml (2 fl oz) extra virgin olive oil

FOR THE HOMMOUS BALILA
175 g (6 oz) chickpeas soaked overnight in double their amount of water

570 ml (1 pint) water

1 tablespoon bicarbonate of soda

TO GARNISH
75 ml (3 fl oz) extra virgin olive oil

1 tablespoon chopped fresh parsley

TO ACCOMPANY
sliced tomatoes

green olives

Broad bean salad

110 ml (4 fl oz) extra virgin olive oil

350 g (12 oz) broad beans (frozen or fresh)

3 cloves garlic, peeled and finely chopped

½ bunch fresh coriander, finely chopped

1 teaspoon ground coriander

1 teaspoon cumin

1 teaspoon granulated sugar

275 ml (10 fl oz) boiling water

50 ml (2 fl oz) lemon juice

1 teaspoon salt

TO GARNISH
lemon wedges

parsley sprigs

This dish can be served hot as a vegetable accompaniment to main dishes or cold as a mezze item (see picture opposite). It is very simple to prepare; frozen broad beans are widely available and can be used in this recipe without any problems. By using frozen beans you can avoid having to shell the fresh ones!

1   In a heavy-bottomed pan, heat the olive oil and then add the broad beans. Fry on a high heat for a few minutes, then add the garlic, the fresh and ground coriander, cumin and sugar and stir well.

2   Lower the heat to medium, add the water, cover and simmer for 20–25 minutes.

3   Check that the beans are tender. When they are, add the salt, lemon juice and cook for a further 2 minutes. Allow to cool.

4   To serve, arrange the mixture on a flat dish. Garnish with lemon wedges and parsley sprigs.

TIPS

•   Frozen beans are easier to use, and you can now get high quality ones from supermarkets.

•   Fresh broad beans can be used when in season. Choose spring broad beans as they have a more delicate flavour.

•   Always add the salt to the beans after they have cooked as adding it earlier stops the beans cooking as quickly or tenderly.

•   Make sure there is still some liquid in the pot when the bean mix has cooked, as this liquid will gradually be absorbed by the beans as they cool, leaving a nice glaze over them.

Vegetarian stuffed vine leaves

This party dish is the vegetarian version of stuffed vine leaves (warak inab meaning 'vine leaves'). It is an essential part of any mezze and is very popular. Its versatility means it can be served on virtually any occasion. Once cooked it keeps very well in the refrigerator. It can also be frozen if you prefer to make this dish in advance. Vine leaves are now fairly easy to get hold of, so I urge you to try this dish – I am sure you will be hooked.

SERVES: 4–6

PREPARATION TIME: at least 60 minutes

COOKING TIME: 1–1½ hours plus 2–3 hours cooling time, and 1 hour for chilling (optional)

FOR THE FILLING

75 g (3 oz) risotto or pudding rice

5 tomatoes, finely chopped

1 teaspoon tomato purée

1 large onion, peeled and finely chopped

½ bunch flat leaf parsley, finely chopped

3 sprigs fresh mint, finely chopped

½ teaspoon dried mint

½ teaspoon cinnamon

½ teaspoon ground allspice

½ teaspoon sumac (see p. 27)

1 teaspoon sugar

½ tablespoon salt

½ teaspoon white pepper

275 ml (10 fl oz) extra virgin olive oil

225 ml (8 fl oz) lemon juice

½ pint cold water

FOR THE VINE LEAVES

275 g (10 oz) vine leaves (see p. 49)

FOR THE BASE OF THE POT

2 tomatoes, roughly sliced

1 potato, roughly sliced

½ onion, roughly sliced

TO MAKE THE FILLING

1 Mix together the rice, tomatoes, tomato purée, onion, parsley, fresh and dried mint, cinnamon, allspice, sumac, sugar, salt, pepper, olive oil and lemon juice. Put the mixture in a colander over a bowl to strain and catch the juices.

TO PREPARE THE VINE LEAVES

2 Prepare the vine leaves as per method on p. 49.

TO STUFF THE VINE LEAVES

3 Take one vine leaf, and put about 1 tablespoon of the mixture that has been straining in the centre. Tuck in the ends of the leaf and roll it over to form a tube. For the smaller leaves, use two together, and for the larger leaves cut them in half.

TO MAKE THE BASE

4 Place the tomatoes, potatoes and onion in a heavy-bottomed pan.

TO COOK THE STUFFED VINE LEAVES

5 Arrange the stuffed vine leaves in tight circles on top of the base vegetables. Press down with a plate. Cover with the rest of the juices that have been reserved from preparing the filling. Add the cold water.

6 Cover the pan and simmer the contents gently on a low heat for 1–1¼ hours.

7 Remove from the heat, remove the lid and allow to stand to cool for at least 2 hours. You can chill the dish for an hour as well if you like.

TO SERVE

8 Arrange the vine leaves on an oval plate, garnish with shredded lettuce and lemon wedges and drizzle with any left over juices.

TIPS

- The quality of the vine leaves is vital to the success of this dish. If you are able to, choose tender young leaves or fresh ones if possible. If you are using fresh leaves, blanch them as above but reduce the cooking time by 20 minutes.

- The stuffed vine leaves should be cooked on a constant and low heat.

- The vine leaves are best prepared and cooked one day in advance of when they are needed, to allow them to chill in the refrigerator.

TO GARNISH
shredded Iceberg lettuce

lemon wedges

YOU WILL ALSO NEED
a side plate and a heavy object such as a can of tomatoes

Mujadarra

SERVES: **6**
PREPARATION TIME: **20 minutes**
COOKING TIME: **50–60 minutes**

225 g (7 oz) green lentils

2 litres (3½ pints) boiling water

110 ml (4 fl oz) extra virgin olive oil

1 onion, peeled and sliced

1 teaspoon granulated sugar

1 teaspoon cumin

½ teaspoon cinnamon

1 teaspoon salt

½ teaspoon white pepper

50 g (2 oz) cooked white rice,
see p. 32

TO GARNISH

2 onions, peeled and finely sliced,
then fried until crisp

50 g (2 oz) pine nuts, sautéed in
1 teaspoon olive oil

TO ACCOMPANY

toasted pitta bread (see pp. 211–12)
and *Fattoush* (see p. 69)

Lentils and rice dip

This lentil dish, which is served cold, is unique in flavour. It is a comfort food, ideal for all ages – even babies – as it is so mild, full of goodness, yet extremely tasty. It can be used as a dip or as an accompaniment to rice and vegetarian dishes. It can be served at a dinner party or a picnic. On a cold winter's day, it is a great supper – all you need is toasted pitta bread and a Fattoush salad.

1 Wash the lentils, and place in a cooking pot. Add the water, bring back to the boil and gently simmer.

2 While the lentils are simmering, heat the olive oil in a frying pan. Add the onion and sugar. Cook until the onions are slightly browned, then add the mixture to the cooking lentils.

3 Cover the pot with a lid, and continue to simmer gently for 40–50 minutes (checking throughout that there is enough water covering the lentils) until they are well cooked.

4 Add cumin, cinnamon, salt and pepper, and cook for further 5–7 minutes.

5 Liquidise the lentils in a food processor or mouli until they are puréed. Then stir in the heated rice (see Tips).

6 To serve, arrange the mixture on a flat dish or plate, and garnish with the fried onion and pine nuts.

TIPS

- Make sure that the lentils you use have not past their sell-by date, as this will affect the cooking time and overall quality of the finished result.

- A mouli is best for liquidising the lentils, as the skins of the lentils are left behind in the sieve – hence the *Mujadarra* will have a smoother, silkier texture.

- Heat the rice through before adding to the lentils, unless you have just freshly cooked it.

Aubergine mousakaa

Mousakaa *is a great standby* mezze *dish. Once cooked it can be served hot with rice. Alternatively, it can be eaten cold as a salad dish or as an accompaniment to roasts and vegetarian dishes.*

TO PREPARE THE AUBERGINES

1 Peel the aubergines, then halve and slice them to a medium thickness.

2 Leave to soak in salted water. Cover with a dish to weigh the aubergines down and leave for a minimum of 30 minutes.

TO PREPARE THE SAUCE

3 In a pan, heat the olive oil. Add the onion and sugar, and cook until the onion is light brown and slightly caramelised. Add the pepper, tomatoes, cinnamon, allspice, nutmeg, salt and pepper. Add the sieved tomatoes and cook the mixture quickly on a medium heat for 10 to 15 minutes.

4 Add the pomegranate syrup, then remove the mixture from the heat.

TO COOK THE AUBERGINES

5 Drain the aubergines, then pat dry using absorbent kitchen paper.

6 Heat the deep-fat fryer to 350°F (180°C). Alternatively heat a little oil in your frying pan.

7 Deep fry the aubergines to a golden colour, but so that they remain firm (see Tips). Remove from the oil using a slotted spoon and place in a colander with a bowl underneath to catch the oil. Leave them to drain for as long as you can (at least an hour).

TO ASSEMBLE THE MOUSAKAA

8 Line your baking dish with the aubergines. Scatter with the chickpeas.

9 Pour the sauce over the top.

10 On top of the sauce, arrange the sliced tomatoes so that they overlap. Sprinkle with cinnamon, sugar, nutmeg, salt and pepper.

11 Bake in the oven for 10–15 minutes, until light brown on top.

TIPS

• Soaking the aubergines in salty water reduces their absorption of oil.

SERVES: **4–5**

PREPARATION TIME: **40 minutes**

COOKING TIME: **20 minutes**

FOR THE AUBERGINES

2 aubergines

bowl of salted water

vegetable oil for deep frying

FOR THE SAUCE

75 ml (3 fl oz) extra virgin olive oil

1 large onion, peeled and sliced

1 teaspoon granulated sugar

1 red pepper, deseeded and finely sliced

4 salad tomatoes, skinned and chopped

1 teaspoon cinnamon

½ teaspoon ground allspice

½ teaspoon freshly grated nutmeg

1 teaspoon salt

1 teaspoon white pepper

225 g (8 oz) tin chopped tomatoes, sieved

1 teaspoon pomegranate syrup (see p. 26)

75 g (3 oz) chickpeas, tinned and drained, or dried, prepared as on p. 49

FOR THE TOPPING

4 beef tomatoes, sliced

½ teaspoon cinnamon

½ teaspoon sugar

½ teaspoon salt

½ teaspoon white pepper

½ teaspoon freshly grated nutmeg

TEMPERATURE
preheat the oven to gas mark 6,
400°F (190°C)

YOU WILL ALSO NEED
a deep-fat fryer or frying pan
a shallow baking dish, 29 x 20 x 4 cm
(12 x 8 x 2 inches)

- When deep-frying the aubergines, make sure that the oil is at a temperature of 300–350°F (180°C) before placing the aubergines in the fryer, because they need to be browned as quickly as possible with the minimum of cooking.

- Serve hot as a main course or cold as a side dish.

Green beans

This cooked vegetable dish is ideal for anyone counting the calories. It is light but very nutritious and great for vegetarians. It can be served hot or cold, travels well and is a great standby as it keeps well in the refrigerator.

Loubieh bizeit

SERVES: 4
PREPARATION TIME: 20 minutes
COOKING TIME: 25 minutes

75 ml (3 fl oz) extra virgin olive oil

450 g (1 lb) whole French green beans, sliced thinly lengthways

2 cloves garlic, peeled and finely chopped

6 salad tomatoes or 4 beef tomatoes, skinned and chopped

½ teaspoon granulated sugar

1 teaspoon salt

½ teaspoon white pepper

½ teaspoon ground allspice

1 teaspoon cinnamon

225 g (8 oz) tin chopped tomatoes, sieved

75 ml (3 fl oz) boiling water

1 In a deep frying pan, heat the oil. Stir in the beans and sauté on a high heat for a few minutes. Add the garlic and continue to sauté for a further few minutes.

2 Add the salad or beef tomatoes, sugar, salt, white pepper, allspice and cinnamon and stir. Lower the heat, cover with a lid and continue to cook for a few minutes.

3 Add the sieved tomatoes and hot water. Leave to cook for 5–10 minutes on a low heat, stirring occasionally, to tenderise the beans.

4 Keep testing them and adjust the flavourings as needed. Once they are tender, simmer the beans for another 5 minutes.

5 Take off the heat and set aside to cool.

6 Serve on a flat plate, as an accompaniment to *mezze* or hot with rice as a main vegetarian dish.

TIPS
- This recipe will work with any kind of green beans, as long as the cooking time is altered according to the variety.

- You can also use frozen beans; add the beans and follow the recipe, reducing the cooking time by 5 minutes.

- Cook the beans and tomatoes on a low heat, so that they create their own juices.

Chilli potatoes

This is the best alternative I know to chips.

1   Heat the deep-fat fryer to 350–375°F (180–190°C). Alternatively, heat a little oil in your frying pan. Wash and pat dry the potatoes, and then fry them until they are golden brown.

2   Remove the potatoes and drain on absorbent kitchen paper.

3   In a frying pan, heat the olive oil and add the garlic, chilli and coriander. Stir these quickly.

4   Add the potatoes, sugar, salt and pepper. Cook until the potatoes are coated in the spices. Then add the lemon juice and Tabasco.

5   To serve, arrange on a flat dish.

TIPS

* Soaking the potatoes is essential as it improves the crunch and reduces the amount of oil absorbed while frying.

* To avoid the potatoes being too hot, you may choose to add either the Tabasco or the chilli rather than using both!

Batata harra

SERVES: **4**

PREPARATION TIME: **20 minutes, plus soaking the potatoes 30 minutes–1 hour**

COOKING TIME: **15 minutes**

2 tablespoons extra virgin olive oil

3 medium potatoes, peeled and diced, then soaked

2 cloves garlic, peeled and finely chopped

½ small green chilli, deseeded and finely chopped (optional)

½ bunch fresh coriander, finely chopped

½ teaspoon granulated sugar

1 teaspoon salt

1 teaspoon white pepper

1 tablespoon lemon juice

a dash of Tabasco

YOU WILL ALSO NEED
a deep-fat fryer or frying pan

Falafel

I know people who'll travel miles for a Falafel sandwich; a good Falafel is better than a hamburger, and is a firm favourite with children. Luckily it is also nourishing, containing fresh ingredients and an interesting combination of flavours.

1   Place the soaked chickpeas and broad beans in a colander and wash thoroughly under running water. Allow to drain.

2   Place the soaked chickpeas and broad beans in a food processor and process until smooth but with some texture. Take out and place in a mixing bowl.

MAKES: **20**

PREPARATION TIME: **20 minutes plus overnight soaking time**

COOKING TIME: **15 minutes**

275 g (10 oz) chickpeas, soaked in 2.3 litres (4 pints) cold water overnight

175 g (6 oz) split broad beans, soaked with the chickpeas overnight

4 cloves garlic, peeled

3 Rinse the bowl of the processor, and process first the garlic, then the onion, the chilli, the coriander and the pepper. Process each ingredient separately. Once processed, add each ingredient to the chickpea and bean mixture.

4 Add the coriander, cumin, bicarbonate of soda, salt and pepper. Mix by hand, adding cold water until these ingredients form a dough-like consistency.

5 Wrap in cling film and refrigerate for 1 hour.

6 Heat the oil in the deep-fat fryer to 350°F (180°C). Alternatively heat a little oil in your frying pan.

7 Using the spoon and mould or your hands, form a doughnut-shaped *Falafel* or form into balls and smooth the surface. See picture opposite for illustration of the finished product.

8 Deep fry the *Falafel* in batches of 5 until they are light brown and crunchy. Drain on absorbent kitchen paper.

9 Serve with *Tahini sauce*.

TIPS

- The vegetables should just be pulsed quickly in the processor, and in the order described to stop the juices and colours mixing.

- If you have a mincer, the ingredients can be minced rather than processed. This gives a better texture to the mixture.

- If you don't have a *Falafel* mould, you can use your hands to shape the mixture roughly into balls.

- The *Falafel* mixture can be frozen in batches before adding the bicarbonate of soda. The bicarbonate of soda can then be added after defrosting and before frying.

- Chilling the *Falafel* before frying is optional, but it is recommended as it makes the mixture more compact and so easier to fry.

- Pierce the finished moulded *Falafel* to form a doughnut shape using the middle finger; this will ensure even cooking and a lighter texture.

- Have ready sliced tomatoes, pickles, shredded lettuce, chopped parsley, sliced radishes and tahini to make great *Falafel* sandwiches!

½ small onion, peeled and finely chopped (or 3 spring onions, chopped)

½ green chilli, deseeded and finely chopped

1 large tablespoon finely chopped fresh coriander

½ red pepper, deseeded and finely chopped

½ teaspoon ground coriander

1 teaspoon cumin

1 teaspoon bicarbonate of soda

1½ teaspoons salt

½ teaspoon white pepper

110 ml (4 fl oz) cold water

YOU WILL ALSO NEED
a *Falafel* mould (see Suppliers p. 18)

a deep-fat fryer or frying pan

TO ACCOMPANY
Tahini sauce (see p. 47)

Lambs' brains

SERVES: **4**

PREPARATION TIME: **15 minutes**

COOKING TIME: **30 minutes, plus cooling time of 30 minutes–1 hour**

8 lambs' brains

½ medium onion, peeled and chopped

2 bay leaves

1 cinnamon stick

1 teaspoon whole cardamom pods

1 teaspoon whole black peppercorns

1.1 litres (2 pints) cold water

FOR THE COATING

50 g (2 oz) plain flour

½ teaspoon ground cinnamon

½ teaspoon salt

½ teaspoon white pepper

TO COOK THE BRAINS

110 ml (4 fl oz) olive oil

FOR THE DRESSING

½ teaspoon granulated sugar

1 teaspoon salt

1 teaspoon Dijon mustard

25 ml (1 fl oz) lemon juice

50 ml (2 fl oz) white wine vinegar

150 ml (5 fl oz) extra virgin olive oil

FOR THE SALAD

1 shredded Iceberg lettuce

TO GARNISH

1 teaspoon chopped fresh parsley

1 spring onion, chopped

lemon wedges

Nkhaat are an unusual delicacy that once discovered will never be forgotten. Their taste is very distinctive, yet the overall texture and flavour when combined with the salad and dressing is very mild. The recipe described here will convert you to this little-known delicacy and familiarise you with this unusual ingredient. Do venture beyond normality, and experience these new flavours.

TO PREPARE THE BRAINS

1 Wash the brains. Then put in a pan with the onion, bay leaves, cinnamon stick, cardamom pods and peppercorns. Cover with cold water, bring gently to a simmer and cook for 10–15 minutes.

2 Remove the brains gently from the pan and place in bowl. Strain the liquid through a sieve over the brains so that it just covers them. Leave to cool.

TO PREPARE THE COATING

3 Mix together the flour, cinnamon, salt and pepper.

4 Remove the cooled brains from their liquid and pat dry with kitchen paper. Then coat gently with the flour mixture.

TO COOK THE BRAINS

5 Heat the olive oil in a pan and add the flour-coated brains. Cook for a maximum of 1 minute on each side.

6 Remove the brains from the pan and drain on absorbent kitchen paper.

TO MAKE THE SALAD

7 Dry the brains and slice each one into 3 pieces. In a screw-top jar, thoroughly mix together the dressing ingredients.

8 Place the shredded lettuce on flat dish, then arrange the brains on the lettuce. Pour over the salad dressing and decorate with parsley, spring onions and lemon wedges, which should be squeezed over the brains before eating.

- For the best results, the brains should be bought as fresh as possible.
- The brains are not as fragile as they look and take shape on cooking. They are easy to work with as long as they are handled gently and with care.
- The brains can be cooked from frozen.

Lambs' tongues

Lsanat *are a very tasty meat with their own distinctive flavour. Their special qualities – unknown to most people – are something I feel need to be promoted, so I have introduced them in my book. There are many ways of using them. However, as an introduction I think a salad is the most suitable. It is very fresh tasting yet subtle and full of body. The only way to find out if you like them is to try them, so I hope you will not let me down.*

TO PREPARE THE TONGUES

1 Put the washed tongues in a pan and cover with the cold water. Add the onion, cardamom pods, allspice or cinnamon stick and peppercorns.

2 Bring to the boil, cover with a lid and allow to simmer gently on a moderate to low heat for 1–1¼ hours. Check the tongues throughout the cooking and do not hesitate to add more water if necessary. The tongues are ready when the outer layer peels off easily.

3 Once they are ready, drain the tongues and reserve their stock.

4 Peel the outer layer from the tongues using gloves or a bowl of cold water in which to dip your hands. Then place them in a clean bowl and cover halfway with the reserved stock. Allow to cool.

5 Mix the salad dressing ingredients together in the screw-top jar.

6 Remove the tongues from the liquid, and slice them thinly lengthways with a sharp knife.

7 Place the tongues on the lettuce. Pour over the salad dressing, and garnish with chopped parsley and spring onions.

8 Chill in the refrigerator for a few minutes if there is time, and then serve.

YOU WILL ALSO NEED
a jar with a screw-top lid

Lsanat

SERVES: **4**

PREPARATION TIME: **30 minutes**

COOKING TIME: **1–1¼ hours, plus minimum cooling time of 1 hour**

FOR THE LAMBS' TONGUES
8 lambs' tongues, washed under cold running water

2.3 litres (4 pints) cold water

½ onion, peeled and chopped

1 teaspoon whole cardamom pods

1 teaspoon ground allspice or 1 cinnamon stick

1 teaspoon whole black peppercorns

FOR THE SALAD
1 shredded Iceberg lettuce to make a bed on the serving dish

FOR THE DRESSING
½ teaspoon Dijon mustard

½ teaspoon salt

½ teaspoon ground black pepper

1 teaspoon mayonnaise

50 ml (2 fl oz) lemon juice

50 ml (2 fl oz) white wine vinegar

75 ml (3 fl oz) extra virgin olive oil

TIPS

- Cooking the tongues is the most crucial part of this recipe. They need to be checked regularly to make sure they are well covered with stock, otherwise they will not become tender.

- Frozen tongues can be used instead of fresh ones, but make sure they are properly defrosted.

- Cover the prepared salad with cling film and chill it after preparation to retain the moisture of the tongues.

Kalawi

Lambs' kidneys

SERVES: **4**
PREPARATION TIME: **20 minutes**
COOKING TIME: **15 minutes**

450 g (1 lb) fresh lambs' kidneys (about 10 kidneys)

4 tablespoons extra virgin olive oil

1 teaspoon salt

½ teaspoon white pepper

½ teaspoon cinnamon

2 large onions, peeled and thinly sliced

½ teaspoon freshly ground black pepper

⅓ teaspoon ground allspice

TO GARNISH
lemon wedges

sprigs of fresh parsley

Lambs' kidneys are a dish in which nutritional value and incredible taste go hand in hand. This dish is a great delicacy, full of vitamins and flavour. The way they are prepared is vital to the final result – the heat of the frying pan is the key to sealing in the flavour as soon as you start to cook them. The kidneys should be caramelised on the outside, yet moist, cooked through and not too heavily spiced so that their natural flavour comes through. I cannot emphasise enough their goodness.

TO PREPARE THE KIDNEYS

1 Clean the kidneys by removing the white outside layer covering each one.

2 Cut each kidney in half longways, and dice each half into 3 pieces. Remove the middle vein and discard.

3 Wash the pieces thoroughly and allow to drain in a colander until ready. Dry them before frying.

TO COOK THE KIDNEYS

4 In a large frying pan, heat the olive oil until hot.

5 Add the kidneys and cook for about 3 minutes on a high heat, shaking the pan to move the kidneys around.

6 Once the kidneys are sealed, lower the temperature to medium and season with salt, white pepper, cinnamon and allspice and cook for 5 minutes more.

7 Add the onion and black pepper and shake the pan (moving around the contents gently). Cook for about 7 minutes until the onions are soft and slightly caramelised.

8 Lower the heat and leave to cook gently for 2 more minutes; the kidneys will then be ready.

9 To serve, place the kidneys on a flat dish, and decorate with lemon wedges and parsley, with or without a salad.

TIPS

• Buy your kidneys from a good butcher as freshness is very important.

• You can add more onions if you like – for this recipe, the more onions, the better!

• Test and taste to make sure the kidneys are cooked through before serving.

Chicken livers

Because of the pomegranate syrup and lemon juice in this recipe, chicken livers cooked the Lebanese way are probably the tastiest you'll come across. This dish is very popular – and rightly so. It is very nutritious and this tasty recipe is simple yet exotic.

1 To clean and prepare the livers, remove the sinew and cut them into equal pieces.

2 In a heavy-bottomed frying pan, heat the vegetable oil, add the chicken livers and cook on a high heat to seal in their juices, shaking the pan to move the livers around. Don't be tempted to use a spoon to stir them – allow them to take shape and become firm. Then you can use a spoon.

3 Lower the heat and allow the livers to sauté covered with a lid to avoid splashes for 5 more minutes.

4 Remove the excess oil from the pan, then season the livers with cinnamon, salt and pepper. Sauté gently together for 3 minutes.

5 Add the pomegranate syrup and simmer gently with the other ingredients for 2 more minutes.

Sawdat dajaj

SERVES: **4**
PREPARATION TIME: **20 minutes**
COOKING TIME: **20 minutes**

75 ml (3 fl oz) vegetable oil

450 g (1 lb) chicken livers, cleaned

½ teaspoon cinnamon

1 teaspoon salt

½ teaspoon white pepper

25 ml (1 fl oz) lemon juice

2 tablespoons pomegranate syrup (see p. 26)

TO GARNISH
sprigs of fresh coriander

6 Add the lemon juice and cook for a further minutes.

7 To serve, place on a plate and decorate with the sprigs of coriander.

TIP

• These days, it's fairly easy to get hold of fresh chicken livers. And the fresher they are, the easier they are to clean.

Sweetbreads

Hlaiwat are a true Lebanese delicacy. Once tried for the first time they can become a craving. The method of cooking is very important – grilling is best as it gives the sweetbreads a full-bodied roasted flavour, coupled with a unique soft texture. A sense of adventure is needed, and once that is achieved, you will certainly be converted!

1 Clean the sweetbreads by removing the sinew and fatty bits that are attached to them; wash and drain in a colander.

2 Thread the sweetbreads on to the skewers.

3 Place the skewers on the tray and under the preheated grill.

4 Turn the skewers after 3 minutes onto their other side, grill for 3 more minutes, then turn again and grill for a further minute so the sweetbreads are cooked through.

5 Switch off the grill, leaving the sweetbreads to dry in the oven for 2 minutes.

6 To serve, remove the sweetbreads from the skewers and place on a large plate. Put each spice carefully in a row on the side of the plate, so that people can dip the sweetbreads into them. Decorate the dish with the sprigs of parsley and have the lemon wedges ready to squeeze over if desired.

Hlaiwat

SERVES: **4**
PREPARATION TIME: **20 minutes**
COOKING TIME: **15 minutes**

350 g (12 oz) sweetbreads, cleaned and cut into halves if they are too big

½ teaspoon chilli powder

½ teaspoon cumin

½ teaspoon sumac (see p. 27)

½ teaspoon salt

½ teaspoon white pepper

TO GARNISH
lemon wedges

sprigs of fresh parsley

TEMPERATURE
preheat the grill to a medium temperature

YOU WILL ALSO NEED
8–10 skewers

an oven tray lined with aluminium foil

TIPS

- Although the sweetbreads can be fried, gentle grilling tenderises them so that they melt in the mouth.

- The spices are very important as they finish off the exotic blend of flavours.

- Sweetbreads freeze very well. When purchased, they should be cleaned before being put into the freezer bags.

PASTRIES

Pastries have a multitude of purposes – ranging from being served on special occasions and throughout the period of Ramadan, to being tucked into a corner of your lunch box. For whatever reason you choose to cook these pastries, and whenever you decide to eat them, one thing remains unchanged – the taste will always leave you wanting more.

MAKES: 24 pieces

PREPARATION TIME: 1 hour

COOKING TIME: 20 minutes

FOR THE PASTRY

50 g (2 oz) plain flour

350 g (12 oz) puff pastry, fresh or frozen

FOR THE FILLING

2 tablespoons ghee or vegetable oil

1 onion, peeled and finely chopped

225 g (8 oz) minced lamb

1 teaspoon salt

1 teaspoon white pepper

1 teaspoon cinnamon

50 g (2 oz) pine nuts, sautéed in 1 teaspoon oil or butter

2 tablespoons *Yoghurt cheese* (see p. 76)

1 tablespoon chopped fresh parsley

2 teaspoons sumac (see p. 27)

TO GARNISH

sprigs of fresh parsley

YOU WILL ALSO NEED

6 cm (2½ inch) pastry cutter

a rolling pin

a deep-fat fryer if not oven-cooking

Meat sambousek

During Ramadan, sambousek is more popular than ever. It is a festive dish, and its mild flavour is loved by children. Once fried it keeps well for a few hours. At parties, buffets and formal or informal gatherings, sambousek must be present! It is very easy to make and can have various fillings.

TO PREPARE THE PASTRY

1 Dust a surface with the plain flour and roll out the pastry to 0.25 cm (⅛ inch) thickness.

2 Using the pastry cutter, cut the pastry into 24 pieces.

3 Arrange the pastry pieces on a tray, cover with cling film and place in the refrigerator while the filling is made.

TO PREPARE THE FILLING

4 Heat the ghee or vegetable oil in a deep frying pan. Add the chopped onion and sauté together stirring continuously until the onions are slightly brown.

5 Add the minced lamb and turn up the heat to high. Stir to separate the meat, and cook until light brown. Add the salt, pepper and cinnamon and mix in thoroughly.

6 Reduce the heat and allow to cook together on a low heat for 5 minutes, stirring occasionally.

7 Add the pine nuts, switch off the heat and set aside.

8 Transfer the mixture to a colander and allow to drain and cool for at least half an hour.

9 Once the filling has cooled, add the *Yoghurt cheese*, parsley and sumac and mix in.

TO ASSEMBLE THE SAMBOUSEK

10 Place a teaspoon of the filling on one side of each pastry circle. Fold the pastry over to form a half moon shape and seal both edges by pressing down with the prongs of a fork.

11 Chill the pastries in the refrigerator for 30 minutes to 1 hour.

TO COOK THE SAMBOUSEK

12 Heat the oil for deep frying to 350°F (180°C). Then fry the *sambousek* in small batches until they are golden in colour. *Meat sambousek* can be baked instead of fried. Arrange the pastries on an oven tray lined with parchment paper, and bake at gas mark 6, 400°F (200°C) for 10–12 minutes.

13 Remove from the oil and drain on dry absorbent kitchen paper.

TO SERVE

14 Arrange the *sambousek* on a flat plate and decorate with parsley sprigs. See picture on the next page.

TIPS

- You can use fresh or frozen pastry, but if you prefer to use frozen, do make sure you follow the instructions for defrosting.

- Make sure that the stuffing is cool before adding the *labneh*.

- It is important to seal the edges on both sides of the pastry so that it cooks evenly on both sides in the shortest possible time.

- The stuffing can be prepared well in advance as it needs to cool.

- When filling the pastry circles, make sure that the edges are not touched by the filling.

- Any leftover pastry can be chilled in the refrigerator and used at a later date.

- The pastries freeze very well, and can be cooked from frozen.

Cheese sambousek

Cheese sambousek *is eaten at any time – for breakfast, as a snack or with lunch or dinner. It is light but nutritious, mild yet tasty. It keeps for longer than the* meat sambousek. *It is very versatile, being suitable for adult or children's parties, and picnics.*

TO PREPARE THE PASTRY

1 Dust surface with flour, roll out the pastry to 0.25 cm (⅛ inch) thick.

2 Using the pastry cutter, cut the pastry into 24 pieces.

3 Arrange the pastry pieces on a tray, cover with cling film and place in the refrigerator while the filling is made.

TO PREPARE THE FILLING

4 In a bowl, place the halloumi, feta and ricotta cheese.

5 Add the egg yolk and parsley, mix the ingredients together.

TO ASSEMBLE THE SAMBOUSEK

6 Place a teaspoon of the filling on to one side of each pastry circle. Fold the pastry over to form a half moon shape and seal both edges by pressing down with the prongs of a fork.

7 Chill the pastries in the refrigerator for 30 minutes to 1 hour.

TO COOK THE SAMBOUSEK

8 Heat the oil for deep frying to 350°F (180°C). Then fry the *sambousek* in small batches until they are golden in colour. Alternatively, to bake in the oven, arrange on an oven tray lined with baking parchment paper and then bake at gas mark 6, 400°F (200°C) for 10–12 minutes.

9 Remove from the oil and drain on absorbent kitchen paper.

TO SERVE

10 Arrange the *sambousek* on a flat plate and decorate with mint sprigs. See picture opposite.

TIP

• Please see the Tips on p. 101. These apply to *Cheese sambousek* as well as meat.

Sambousek jibneh

MAKES: **24 pieces**

PREPARATION TIME: **1 hour**

COOKING TIME: **20 minutes**

FOR THE PASTRY

50 g (2 oz) plain flour

350 g (12 oz) puff pastry, fresh or frozen

FOR THE FILLING

75 g (3 oz) halloumi cheese, quickly pulsed in a food processor

25 g (1 oz) feta cheese, crumbled

75 g (3 oz) ricotta cheese

1 egg yolk

1 tablespoon chopped fresh parsley

TO GARNISH

sprigs of fresh mint

YOU WILL ALSO NEED

6 cm (2½ inch) pastry cutter

a rolling pin

a deep-fat fryer if not oven cooking

Spinach pastries

Fatayer contains spinach, and I promise you that spinach has never been used for a better purpose. This pastry is creamy, lemony, spinachy ... what more could you ask for?

MAKES: 36 pieces
PREPARATION TIME: 45 minutes
COOKING TIME: 20 minutes

FOR THE PASTRY
3 g (½ sachet) active dried yeast or 1 teaspoon fresh yeast

1 teaspoon granulated sugar

175 ml (6 fl oz) warm water

225 g (8 oz) plain flour, sifted

1 teaspoon salt

50 g (2 oz) unsalted butter, diced and at room temperature

FOR THE FILLING
250 g (9 oz) fresh spinach, finely chopped

½ large onion, peeled and finely chopped

1 teaspoon salt

½ teaspoon white pepper

1 tablespoon sumac (see p. 27)

½ teaspoon thyme (see p. 28) (optional)

½ tablespoon pomegranate syrup (see p. 26)

50 ml (2 fl oz) extra virgin olive oil

25 ml (1 fl oz) lemon juice

25 g (1 oz) pine nuts, sautéed in 25 ml (1 fl oz) olive oil

TO GARNISH
lemon wedges

YOU WILL ALSO NEED
6 cm (2½ inch) pastry cutter

2 baking trays, lined with baking parchment

TO PREPARE THE PASTRY

1 Put the yeast, sugar and warm water in a bowl and mix. Cover and leave for 3–4 minutes.

2 Put the flour and salt in a food processor and mix slowly.

3 Add the butter and mix for 1 to 2 minutes until it is combined with the flour. Your mixture should now resemble fine breadcrumbs.

4 Pour the yeast mixture through the feed tube, and continue to mix until it forms a ball of dough.

5 Remove your dough from the processor, place in a bowl, cover in cling film and allow it to rest for 15 minutes.

TO PREPARE THE FILLING

6 Place the chopped spinach in a bowl, add the onion and salt; mix these ingredients together well.

7 Squeeze out any juice from the mixture by forming into balls while squeezing. Then return to a clean bowl.

8 Add the pepper, sumac, thyme (if using), pomegranate syrup, olive oil and lemon juice. Mix the ingredients together.

9 Transfer the mixture to a colander and squeeze out as much liquid as possible.

10 Place the mixture back into a bowl, and add the pine nuts.

TO ASSEMBLE THE FATAYER

11 Put the pastry between the two polythene bags and roll out evenly to a thickness of ¼ cm.

12 Using a pastry cutter, cut the pastry into circles.

13 Place a teaspoonful of the filling in the middle of the pastry circle. Shape the pastry like a three-cornered hat, then seal the joins using your fingertips.

14 Repeat with the rest of the circles and filling, making sure that the filling does not touch the edge of the circle.

TO COOK THE FATAYER

14 Place on the baking trays and cook in the oven for 10–15 minutes.

TO SERVE

15 Allow to cool, then place on an oval dish and garnish with lemon wedges.

TIPS

- The spinach needs to be squeezed well to remove any liquid before filling the pastry, otherwise the liquid will be trapped and open the seal on the edges and spoil the shape of the pastry.

- Do not over-bake, as the pastry should retain its softness and never brown.

- When assembling the *Fatayer*, make sure that your fingertips are free of the filling mixture as otherwise the edges will not seal properly and will open up during cooking. Have a cloth ready to clean your fingers after preparing each one.

- Bake one tray at a time, to ensure they are all equally cooked.

- The pastries can be frozen in polythene bags and defrosted when needed.

a rolling pin

2 polythene bags

TEMPERATURE
preheat the oven to gas mark 4, 350°F (180°C)

MEZZE: MEAT DISHES

All of the recipes in this section use lamb as their basic ingredient. The first explains fully how you can best prepare raw lamb fillet. The subsequent recipes give various ways of adding to and flavouring this important basic ingredient. In some the meat remains uncooked. In others, it is fried or grilled. Whatever the method of preparation, here are some excellent *mezze* dishes which can be served with a variety of accompaniments.

Habra

SERVES: **4**

PREPARATION TIME: **40 minutes**

2 shoulders of lamb, boned (ask your
butcher to do this)

YOU WILL ALSO NEED
a food processor

Preparation of lamb fillet

*Habra (raw lamb fillet) is really at the heart of Lebanese cuisine. It is truly
majestic and in a class of its own. The meat itself needs to be prepared and
chilled for a minimum of 2 hours, and can even be prepared one day in
advance. The* habra, *once prepared, requires little effort to serve as* Habra
nayyeh, Kafta nayyeh *or* Kibbeh nayyeh. Habra *is also needed to prepare*
Kibbeh maklieh, Kibbeh meshweyeh *and* Kibbeh bisineyeh. *The message
that I want to convey is that all these dishes are connected. Once the
logistics are taken on board, the rest is easy. The first time you make* habra
will be the hardest, but it does become easier. Remember that habra *is the
foundation for all these recipes.*

TO PREPARE THE LAMB

1 Take the upper face of the boned shoulder of lamb and cut the meat
   into pieces. Remove as many veins and as much sinew and fat as
   possible from the lamb pieces. Repeat with the other boned shoulder.

2 Place the meat in your food processor, and process until the meat is
   completely ground, so it resembles pâté.

3 Separate the habra into 2 parts and cover each with cling film.
   Freeze one half for future use, and chill the other half in the
   refrigerator.

4 The *habra* should weigh about 550 g (1¼ lb).

Habra nayyeh

1 Place the prepared, chilled lamb fillet on a clean board and add the salt and pepper and mix gently and carefully.

2 Divide the mixture into four parts.

3 Grease the palm of your hand with a little olive oil, and gently rub each piece against the board to form a cylindrical (sausage) shape.

4 Using a large-bladed knife, flatten each piece to form a ridged pattern.

TO SERVE

5 Lay on a serving dish and garnish with mint sprigs and *Tabla*.

TIPS

• Removing as many veins as possible improves the texture of the final result.

• Always work with the fingertips, applying a minimum of pressure so as not to alter the temperature of meat.

• Olive oil can be drizzled on the *Habra nayyeh* just before serving.

SERVES: **4**

PREPARATION TIME: **15 minutes**

1 quantity of prepared lamb fillet, chilled (see p. 108)

1 teaspoon salt

½ teaspoon white pepper

25 ml (1 fl oz) extra virgin olive oil

YOU WILL ALSO NEED
a large-bladed knife

a wooden or marble board

TO ACCOMPANY
Tabla (see p. 46)

sprigs of fresh mint

Kibbeh nayyeh

Kibbeh nayyeh *is an enhancement of the basic* Habra nayyeh *recipe (see above) through the addition of burgul and herbs, and, as with* Habra nayyeh, *the meat needs to be prepared a day in advance and then chilled. This version is more popular because it has more to it than just the raw meat flavour. A true experience, which needs to be savoured.*

1 Place the ̄Habra nayyeh into a bowl. Into it, mix the burgul, mint, spring onion, cumin, salt and pepper. Taste and adjust seasoning as necessary.

2 Divide the mixture into 4 parts.

3 Grease the palm of your hand with olive oil and gently roll each piece against your clean board to form a cylindrical (sausage) shape.

4 Using a large-bladed knife, flatten each piece and form a ridged pattern.

SERVES: **4**

PREPARATION TIME: **40 minutes**

FOR THE RAW KIBBEH
Half quantity of prepared *Habra nayyeh* (see above)

40 g (1½ oz) brown or white burgul, washed twice, leaving behind a little water to soften it further – set aside for at least 30 minutes so it fluffs up

6 fresh mint leaves, finely chopped

1 spring onion, finely chopped

¼ teaspoon cumin

1 teaspoon salt

1 teaspoon white pepper

25 ml (1 fl oz) olive oil

FOR THE TABLA

75 g (3 oz) *Tabla* (see p. 46)

½ teaspoon sumac (see p. 27)

50 ml (2 fl oz) olive oil

TO GARNISH

25 g (1 oz) pine nuts

mint sprigs

YOU WILL ALSO NEED

a large-bladed knife

a wooden or marble board

5 To prepare the *Tabla*, mix together the above ingredients with sumac and olive oil.

TO SERVE

6 Place the *Kibbeh nayyeh* on a serving dish with the *Tabla* mix at one side. Garnish with pine nuts and mint sprigs and serve immediately.

TIPS

- The meat and burgul need to be chilled as the temperature of these ingredients affects the result.

- Always work with the fingertips, applying a minimum of pressure so as not to alter the temperature of meat.

- Dip the tip of the large-bladed knife in olive oil as it makes the task of shaping the pieces easier.

- Traditionally, *Kibbeh nayyeh* and *Habra nayyeh* are served together on a large platter so both can be prepared for the same occasion.

- *Kibbeh nayyeh* should not be too spicy or overpowering. Its flavour should be mild, with the freshness and quality of the meat coming through thanks to the careful handling of the ingredients.

- Any left over mixture can also be cooked as per *Kibbeh meshweyehj*, see p. 116 – from step 2.

SERVES: **4**

PREPARATION TIME: **40 minutes**

FOR THE KAFTA NAYYEH

Half quantity of prepared *Habra nayyeh* (see p. 109)

1 small onion, peeled and very finely chopped

¼ small red pepper, deseeded and very finely chopped

1 tablespoon chopped fresh parsley

Kafta nayyeh

Here is a third recipe that uses the basic Habra nayyeh *mixture described on p. 109. The chopped onions and peppers added to the mixture make it more chunky than both the original version and* Kibbeh nayyeh *(pp. 109–10).* Habra nayyeh, Kibbeh nayyeh *and* Kafta nayyeh *served together on a wooden board make up the ultimate Lebanese mezze.*

TO PREPARE THE KAFTA NAYYEH

1 To the basic *Habra nayyeh* mixture add the onion, pepper, parsley, salt and pepper. Mix well.

2 Divide the mixture into 4 parts.

1 teaspoon salt

½ teaspoon white pepper

25 ml (1 fl oz) olive oil

FOR THE TABLA

75 g (3 oz) *Tabla* (see p. 46)

½ teaspoon sumac (see p. 27)

50 ml (2 fl oz) olive oil

TO GARNISH

25 g (1 oz) pine nuts

a few sprigs of fresh parsley

3 Grease the palm of your hand with olive oil and gently roll each piece against your clean board to form a cylindrical (sausage) shape.

4 Using a large-bladed knife, flatten each piece to form a ridged pattern.

TO PREPARE THE TABLA

5 Mix together the *Tabla* ingredients with sumac and olive oil.

TO SERVE

6 Place the *Kafta nayyeh* on a serving dish with the *Tabla* mix to one side. Garnish with pine nuts and parsley sprigs.

TIPS

- The finer the onions and pepper are chopped, the better the finished result.
- Always work with the fingertips, applying a minimum of pressure so as not to alter the temperature of meat.
- It is vital to serve these raw meat dishes as soon as they are prepared, as otherwise the meat discolours and will lose its fresh taste.

Kibbeh makleih

MAKES: **28–30 *Kibbeh makleih***

PREPARATION TIME: **1½ hours plus overnight soaking of burgul**

COOKING TIME: **40 minutes**

FOR THE KIBBEH MAKLEIH BALLS

1 small onion, peeled and roughly chopped

275 g (10 oz) brown burgul washed, drained and left in enough cold water to moisten it overnight in the refrigerator, covered in cling film

Half quantity of prepared *Habra nayyeh* (see p. 109)

This recipe is basically a ball of Kibbeh nayyeh, which is then stuffed with a flavoursome filling and deep fried. It may sound complicated and difficult, but with practice it's easy enough to develop the skills needed to make this dish. The trick is to get the right consistency for the ball itself, because then it will hold the filling and keep its shape.

USING THE HABRA NAYYEH TO PREPARE THE KIBBEH MAKLEIH BALLS

1 Put the onion into the food processor and process until very fine. Add the burgul to the processor and process for a few minutes with the onions. Add the *Habra nayyeh*, salt, pepper, cumin and cinnamon and blend together for about 2 minutes.

2 Transfer to a bowl, cover with cling film and refrigerate.

TO PREPARE THE FILLING

3 Meanwhile, in a deep frying pan, heat the olive oil or ghee. Add the onions and sugar, and mix thoroughly on a high heat until slightly browned.

4 Add the lamb mince to the onions, keeping the high heat until the meat is slightly browned.

5 Reduce the heat to moderate, add the salt, pepper, cinnamon and allspice and mix well. Fry together for a few minutes, then switch off the heat and set aside to cool.

6 Once the filling cools, add the sumac and the pine nuts.

TO ASSEMBLE THE KIBBEH BALLS

7 Take the prepared mixture from the refrigerator.

8 Grease the palms of your hands with olive oil. Take small pieces of mixture and roll into balls of approximately 3 cm (1¼ inch) diameter – about the size of a walnut.

9 Using your forefinger, create a hole as wide as possible in each of the balls. Place a small amount of filling in these cavities, then seal.

10 Grease your palms with olive oil and shape the sealed *kibbeh* balls as shown in the picture (see p. 114). Alternatively, as long as the balls are well sealed, you can shape them however you like.

11 Chill the *kibbeh*s for a minimum of 1 hour.

TO COOK

12 When you are ready to cook the *kibbeh*s, preheat the deep-fat fryer to 375°F (190°C) and fry in batches. Drain on absorbent kitchen paper.

TO SERVE

13 Put the balls on a plate and garnish with the lemon wedges, which can be squeezed over them.

TIPS

• Soaking the brown burgul overnight is essential as it creates the right texture to blend with the meat. If using white burgul, the overnight process is not necessary as white burgul is finer; washing it and then draining is enough. Remember that brown burgul has a nuttier flavour.

1 teaspoon salt

1 teaspoon white pepper

1 teaspoon cumin

1 teaspoon cinnamon

FOR THE FILLING
2 tablespoons olive oil or ghee

1 medium onion, peeled and finely chopped

½ teaspoon granulated sugar

225 g (8 oz) minced lamb

1 teaspoon salt

1 teaspoon white pepper

½ teaspoon cinnamon

½ teaspoon ground allspice

1 tablespoon sumac (see p. 27)

50 g (2 oz) pine nuts

TO GARNISH
lemon wedges

YOU WILL ALSO NEED
a deep-fat fryer

- Chilling the blended mixture is vital because it helps in the overall preparation.

- The filling needs to be cool before using.

- Do not over-grease your hands with oil, or they will become too slippery.

- The final *kibbeh*s can be chilled on a tray before frying or frozen for later use. (They can be stored in the freezer for as long as 6 months.)

- The number of the *kibbeh*s will vary according to their size, so try to stick to the size and number suggested.

- If you want to make fewer *kibbeh*, halve the amounts in the recipe — it will work just as well.

Kibbeh makhtoum

This recipe is basically the same as for Kibbeh makleih, *but with a vegetarian stuffing. Once again I created this stuffing for my client, Sheikh Mohammed Bin Rashid al-Makhtoum. In fact, when I first made it, I loved it so much it has now become my star* kibbeh. *Please try it. It's very good.*

TO PREPARE THE STUFFING

1 In a deep frying pan on a moderate heat, heat the olive oil. Add to it the chopped ginger, then the onion and sugar, and stir until light brown.

2 Add the carrot, mushrooms, salt, pepper, cinnamon and cumin and stir gently.

3 Add the frozen peas, spinach and coriander, stirring continuously. Add the pine nuts and turn off the heat.

4 Add the pomegranate syrup and sumac, and then transfer the mixture to a colander to drain off any oil.

5 Leave the mixture to cool before filling the *kibbeh* balls.

TO ASSEMBLE AND COOK THE KIBBEH MAKHTOUM

6 Stuff the *kibbeh* balls with the cooled mixture, as with the *Kibbeh makleih* recipe pp. 112–13, following steps 7–11 inclusive.

7 Fry the *kibbeh* as in the *Kibbeh makleih* recipe, step 12.

8 Serve the *kibbeh* on a plate garnished with lemon wedges which can be squeezed over them.

TIPS

• You can freeze these *kibbeh* as before. Defrost in the refrigerator for 4–6 hours or preferably overnight before using.

• *Kibbeh* can be fried from frozen, but ensure that the filling is cooked through.

• The vegetables should be fried gradually on a moderate heat, so that they are not overcooked.

MAKES: **28–30 *Kibbeh makhtoum***

PREPARATION TIME: **1½ hours, plus overnight soaking of burgul**

COOKING TIME: **20 minutes**

FOR THE KIBBEH BALLS
Follow the ingredients list and the method for *Kibbeh makleih* (see pp. 112–13) steps 1–6 inclusive, and refresh your memory of the method by looking at the Tips.

FOR THE STUFFING
25 ml (2 fl oz) extra virgin olive oil

25 g (1 oz) root ginger, peeled and finely chopped

1 onion, peeled and chopped

1 teaspoon granulated sugar

1 carrot, peeled and finely sliced

50 g (2 oz) mushrooms, finely sliced

1 teaspoon salt

½ teaspoon white pepper

1 teaspoon cinnamon

½ teaspoon cumin

50 g (2 oz) frozen peas (petit pois)

50 g (2 oz) fresh spinach, finely chopped

1 tablespoon chopped fresh coriander

25 g (1 oz) pine nuts

½ tablespoon pomegranate syrup (see p. 26)

1 teaspoon sumac (see p. 27)

TO GARNISH
lemon wedges

YOU WILL ALSO NEED
a deep-fat fryer

Kibbeh meshweyehj

Kibbeh meshweyehj is an ideal mezze accompaniment. It is lean, with a minimum of fat – grilling is the best way to cook it. It is served as a main course with white rice and a salad, or as an accompaniment to grills as an alternative to kebabs.

MAKES: **12 skewers**

PREPARATION TIME: **40 minutes, plus overnight soaking of burgul**

COOKING TIME: **15 minutes**

Half quantity of prepared *Habra nayyeh* (see p. 109)

50 g (2 oz) brown burgul, washed twice, leaving behind a little water to soften it further – set aside for at least 30 minutes so it fluffs up

½ teaspoon cumin

50 g (2 oz) pine nuts

1 teaspoon salt

1 teaspoon white pepper

FOR GRILLING

2 fl oz (25 ml) extra virgin olive oil

YOU WILL ALSO NEED

skewers for grilling

a griddle

an oven tray lined with foil

TEMPERATURE

preheat the grill to a medium temperature

TO PREPARE THE KIBBEH MESHWEYEHJ

1 On a clean chopping board, mix together the *Habra nayyeh* with the burgul, cumin, pine nuts, salt and pepper. Blend well by hand, form into a ball and set aside.

2 Divide the ball into 12 pieces.

3 Skewer each piece and brush with olive oil.

TO COOK

4 Place the skewers on a griddle and cook for one minute on each side to brown.

5 Transfer the skewers to the waiting oven tray, and once all the skewers have been griddled, place the tray under the grill.

6 Grill for 4 minutes, turning regularly.

TO SERVE

7 Remove from the grill and bring to the waiting crowd (hopefully!): this *kibbeh* won't wait for anybody!

8 Serve with *Cucumber and yoghurt salad* (pp. 34–5), *Aubergine dip* (p. 74) and *White rice* (p. 32) or other *mezze* dishes of your choice.

TIPS

- Any leftover *Kibbeh nayyeh* mixture (see pp. 109–10) can also be used for this recipe. Proceed from step 2.

- *Kibbeh meshweyehj* can be prepared in advance, ready to put onto skewers for cooking when required.

- Brushing the skewers with olive oil is optional, but will keep the *kibbeh* moist while cooking.

- Melted butter can be used instead of olive oil, but in these health-conscious times, olive oil is a better option.

Kibbeh laban

This is a substantial dish, and a firm family favourite. The various flavours were made for each other, and with rice as an accompaniment this is perfect comfort food.

TO COOK THE YOGHURT

1 In a medium-sized pan, blend together the yoghurt and water. Add the salt and pepper and heat gently, stirring continuously to avoid curdling and until the sauce begins to boil.

2 Just as the mixture reaches boiling point, add the cornflour paste to thicken. Continue to stir, simmer it on a low, gentle heat for a few minutes.

3 Meanwhile, in a small frying pan, heat the ghee or clarified butter. Once it is hot, add the garlic and sauté slowly and gently. Then add the coriander and fry quickly together.

4 Transfer this mixture to the pan containing the simmering yoghurt sauce.

5 Add the fried *kibbeh* to the yoghurt sauce, stir and switch off the heat.

6 Serve with plain boiled rice.

TIPS

- Traditionally, an egg is also used in the yoghurt sauce. However, I find this method is rich enough – especially if the yoghurt is creamy.

- You can blanch the *kibbeh* in boiling water and then add them to the yoghurt sauce; however, I prefer to fry them as explained in the previous recipe.

SERVES: **4–5**

PREPARATION TIME: **1 hour**

COOKING TIME: **30 minutes**

FOR THE KIBBEH BALLS
Follow the ingredients list and the method for *Kibbeh makleih* (see pp. 112–13), but halving the amount of ingredients to make 14–15 *kibbeh* balls. Follow the method up to and including the frying stage (see steps 1–12), and refresh your memory by looking at the Tips.

FOR THE YOGHURT SAUCE (LABAN)
900 ml (1½ pints) plain yoghurt – preferably home-made, see p. 34, or use Greek yoghurt

300 ml (½ pint) water

1 teaspoon salt

½ teaspoon white pepper

1 tablespoon cornflour, blended with 25 ml (1 fl oz) water to form a paste

1 tablespoon ghee or clarified butter

3 cloves garlic, peeled and finely chopped or crushed

1 tablespoon chopped fresh coriander

MAIN DISHES

The dishes in this chapter are wholesome, hearty and nutritious. The list of ingredients and the method may often seem long and complicated, but the steps are easy to follow, and, once you get the hang of it, you won't look back. Elements of the preparation (for example the stuffing) can often be done in advance. And many of the dishes are cooked in the oven, which means there is no last-minute panic before meal times. When they are served with their various sauces and accompaniments, these Lebanese meals look absolutely wonderful. I do hope you enjoy them.

Chicken with molokia leaves

Molokia is cooked all over the Middle East. However, I like to think that the Lebanese version makes the most of the molokia leaves through the delicate preparation required. Molokia leaves are similar to large mint leaves, but are thicker and tougher. And whatever you cook them with, the leaves will always be the star of the recipe. In the UK, fresh molokia leaves are available in the summer months. However, the dried leaves are a good alternative and can be found in most Middle Eastern and Arabic supermarkets.

SERVES: **4**

PREPARATION TIME: **30 minutes**

COOKING TIME: **1–1¼ hours**

FOR THE CHICKEN AND THE STOCK

75 ml (3 fl oz) extra virgin olive oil

1 whole chicken, cleaned, washed and dried

2.3 litres (4 pints) boiling water

4 whole cardamom pods

4 whole black peppercorns

1 lemon slice

½ onion, peeled

1 teaspoon salt

FOR THE MOLOKIA

900 g (2 lb) fresh molokia leaves (washed, drained and with the stalks removed), or 450 g (1 lb) dried molokia (see Tips)

3 tablespoons vegetable oil or ghee

4 cloves garlic, peeled and very finely chopped or ground

2 bunches fresh coriander, finely chopped

the prepared chicken stock

2 teaspoons ground coriander

1 teaspoon sugar

1 tablespoon salt

½ teaspoon white pepper

50 ml (2 fl oz) lemon juice

FOR THE LEMON AND ONION SAUCE

½ onion, very finely chopped

110 ml (4 fl oz) lemon juice

TO PREPARE THE CHICKEN STOCK

1 In a large pan, heat the olive oil. Add the chicken and quickly brown on all sides. This should take about 10 minutes on a high heat. Then add the boiling water, cardamom pods, peppercorns, lemon slice, onion and salt. Bring to the boil, then reduce the heat to moderate, cover with a lid and allow to simmer and cook for 40–50 minutes.

2 Check the chicken to make sure it is cooked. Once it is, strain the stock into a large jug and put to one side. Take the chicken out of the pot and leave it on a plate or tray to cool.

3 When the chicken is cool enough, cut it into chunky pieces, arrange on a tray and cover with foil until required.

TO PREPARE THE MOLOKIA

4 Chop the prepared *molokia* leaves carefully to avoid bruising them.

5 In the large pan you used for making the stock, heat 2 tablespoons of vegetable oil or ghee, then add half the garlic and half of the chopped fresh coriander, and stir quickly.

6 Add the prepared molokia leaves and cook the ingredients gently together for a couple of minutes.

7 Add the chicken stock to the *molokia* mixture. Then add the ground coriander, sugar, salt and pepper, and allow to simmer for about 20 minutes.

8 Meanwhile, heat the remaining ghee or oil in a small frying pan. Add the remaining garlic and chopped coriander, and stir together. Pour into the *molokia* mixture. Taste and adjust as required, add the lemon juice and switch off the heat.

FOR THE VINEGAR AND
ONION SAUCE
½ onion, finely chopped

110 ml (4 fl oz) white wine vinegar

TO ACCOMPANY
White rice (see p. 32)

toasted pitta breads (see p. 211) or
croutons (see p. 33)

lemon and onion sauce

vinegar and lemon sauce

TO SERVE

9 Serve the *molokia* in bowls with the chicken pieces placed in the centre. Plain boiled rice is the perfect accompaniment, and with the toasted pittas and two sauces on the side, it is a meal fit for an emperor! Bon appetit!

FOR THE LEMON AND ONION SAUCE

10 Mix together the ingredients and serve in a bowl on the side.

FOR THE VINEGAR AND ONION SAUCE

11 Mix together the ingredients and serve in a bowl on the side.

TIPS

- If you can't get hold of fresh *molokia*, use the dried version. Dried *molokia* has to be cleaned and then boiled for 20 minutes to tenderise the leaves. Rinse, drain, and then continue as with fresh *molokia*.

- Cut the chicken into chunks rather than slices as this will give an authentic touch. You can protect your hands with oven gloves.

- Don't forget to heat the chicken pieces through before serving.

- The accompaniments are not a must but they are very traditional and Lebanese.

Spinach stew

Spinach is available fresh throughout the year, so this recipe can be an alternative to the molokia dish described previously as it is very similar, and just as nutritious and delicious. It is probably easier to cook and achieve the required result as the ingredients are much more widely available. Try to introduce it very early in life to the youngsters, as it is a dish that grows on you, and erases the myth that spinach is boring.

TO PREPARE THE POULTRY AND THE STOCK

1 In a large pan, heat the oil. Add the poussin or chicken pieces and brown on all sides. Add the boiling water, cardamom pods, peppercorns, lemon slice, onion and salt. Bring to the boil, then reduce to a simmer and cook on a moderate heat for 30 minutes, 40 minutes if using chicken.

2 Check the poussins or chicken to make sure it is cooked. Drain the stock into a large jug and put aside. Place the poussin or chicken pieces in a covered dish until they are needed.

TO PREPARE THE SPINACH

3 Heat the ghee or butter in a large pan. Add the garlic followed by the fresh coriander and fry together quickly for a minute. Then add the spinach and sauté together gently and swiftly.

4 Add the reserved stock, followed by the salt, pepper, ground coriander and sugar.

5 Add the poussin pieces and allow to cook together for 10 minutes, adjusting the seasoning and adding a little more water if necessary.

6 Add the lemon juice, switch off the heat and serve.

TIPS

• The amount of spinach used can altered; the more spinach used, the thicker the result. Personally, I prefer a thicker stew.

• Chicken can be used but I feel that poussins are more delicate and appropriate to serve with the tender spinach. If chicken is used allow more time for cooking.

Yakhnet sabanech

SERVES: **4**
PREPARATION TIME: **20 minutes**
COOKING TIME: **1 hour**

FOR THE POULTRY AND THE STOCK
75 ml (3 fl oz) olive oil

2 poussins, cleaned, washed and jointed, or 6 chicken thigh portions

2.3 litres (4 pints) boiling water

1 teaspoon whole cardamom pods

1 teaspoon whole black peppercorns

1 lemon slice

½ onion, peeled

1 teaspoon salt

FOR THE SPINACH
4 tablespoons vegetable ghee or 75 g (3 oz) butter

4 cloves garlic, crushed

1 bunch fresh coriander leaves, finely chopped

900 g (2 lb) fresh spinach, roughly chopped

the prepared poussin stock

1 teaspoon salt

1 teaspoon white pepper

1 teaspoon ground coriander

½ teaspoon granulated sugar

75 ml (3 fl oz) lemon juice

TO ACCOMPANY
White rice (see p. 32)

FOR THE MARINADE
2 cloves garlic, peeled and finely chopped

1 tablespoon salt

1 teaspoon white pepper

1 teaspoon ground cardamom

1 teaspoon granulated sugar

½ teaspoon cinnamon

25 ml (1 fl oz) lemon juice

50 ml (2 fl oz) extra virgin olive oil

FOR THE CHICKEN
1 chicken, cleaned and dried

1 whole lemon

2 carrots, washed

1 onion, peeled and quartered

4 whole black peppercorns

4 whole cardamom pods

900 ml (1½ pints) boiling water

50 g (2 oz) unsalted butter

FOR THE STUFFING
2 tablespoons ghee or corn oil

1 onion, finely chopped

1 teaspoon granulated sugar

225 g (8 oz) lamb, coarsely minced

1 teaspoon saffron

1 teaspoon ground cardamom

½ teaspoon ground allspice

½ teaspoon cinnamon

1½ teaspoons salt

Stuffed chicken

This is an absolutely delicious way to cook chicken. In fact, the title 'stuffed chicken' may be a bit misleading, because the rice mixture forms a bed for the bird rather than being stuffed into it. It is very popular at the restaurant and a great family dish. To summarise, the order of cooking should be as follows: start to cook the chicken first; then after 45 minutes start cooking the rice so that just as the chicken is coming out of the oven, you are ready to put the rice in. Carve the chicken and make the gravy while the rice is finishing off cooking. Then everything will be hot and ready together for when you serve.

TO PREPARE THE MARINADE

1 Put the garlic, salt, pepper, cardamom, sugar, cinnamon, lemon juice and oil in a blender or small food processor and combine for a few seconds.

2 Rub the marinade all over the chicken, covering as much of the surface as you can, and inside the cavity.

TO COOK THE CHICKEN

3 Place the marinated chicken in a roasting tin. Pour over any marinade that is left.

4 Put the whole lemon in the cavity of the chicken. Place the carrots, onion, peppercorns and cardamom pods around the chicken and pour in the boiling water. Dice the butter and put knobs of it all over the chicken.

5 Cover the whole roasting tin with a double layer of aluminium foil or a lid. Cook in a preheated oven for 1 hour, checking halfway.

6 When the chicken is completely cooked, take it out of the oven and drain off the juices from the roasting tin and reserve them to use later in the gravy.

TO MAKE THE STUFFING

7 Meanwhile, heat the ghee or corn oil in a medium-sized pan. Add the chopped onion and sugar and sauté on a high heat until the onions are light brown.

8 Add the lamb mince and fry with the onions until the meat turns light brown.

½ teaspoon white pepper

900 ml (1½ pints) boiling water

50 g (2 oz) unsalted butter

450 g (1 lb) basmati rice, soaked in 570 ml (1 pint) of boiling water for 5 minutes, then drained, rinsed under hot running water, then drained again in a colander

FOR THE GRAVY

the juices from the roast chicken

25 ml (1 fl oz) lemon juice

a little hot water, if required

1 tablespoon cornflour, blended in 25 ml (1 fl oz) of cold water

25 ml (1 fl oz) double cream

TO GARNISH

pine nuts

TEMPERATURE

preheat the oven to gas mark 7, 425°F (220°C)

YOU WILL ALSO NEED

a roasting tin

an ovenproof saucepan

TO ACCOMPANY

Olive salad (see p. 72)

Home-made yoghurt (see p. 34)

9 Add the saffron, cardamom, allspice, cinnamon, salt and pepper and fry together for a further 2 minutes.

10 Lower the heat, add the water and butter, and allow all the ingredients to come to the boil gently.

11 Leave the mixture to simmer for 5 minutes, then add the rice. Stir once, then cover with a lid and allow the rice to absorb some of the liquid for 2 minutes.

12 Put the pan into the heated oven and leave to finish cooking for 10 minutes. Then remove from the oven and set aside.

TO MAKE THE GRAVY

13 Pour the juices that you reserved from the roasting pan into a saucepan. Add to these the lemon juice and some water if necessary. Bring to the boil.

14 Add the cornflour mixture carefully (you may not need it all), and continue to stir until the sauce thickens. Add the double cream and stir. Cook for a few seconds and then set aside.

TO SERVE

15 Lay your rice mixture on a large platter. Cut the chicken into four pieces and place them on top, and sprinkle with pine nuts. Don't forget your gravy, which should be served on the side in a jug.

TIPS

- The chicken can be marinated well in advance, even overnight, and left in the refrigerator before putting in roasting tin.

- If you are boning the chicken, cut into big chunks to give the dish a rustic look. This is easiest when the chicken is hot, so wear cooking gloves for protection.

Stuffed courgettes

Courgettes filled with lamb are a must: not only are they very traditional in Lebanese cooking but they are also a universal favourite. They might seem tedious to prepare, but the same method can be used for many other vegetables so it's good to practice the technique. Arabic courgettes are ideal for this dish, which you can get from Middle Eastern grocers, but English courgettes are a good enough substitute.

TO PREPARE THE STUFFING

1   In a large bowl mix together the lamb, rice, allspice, salt, pepper, cinnamon, pine nuts and oil and set aside.

TO PREPARE AND STUFF THE COURGETTES

2   Core the courgettes, leaving one end intact to hold in the filling. Put the cored courgettes aside in the bowl of salted water. When they are all done, rinse them under a running tap and drain. Then stuff them with the meat and rice mixture, pushing it gently into the cavity with your forefinger. Leave a gap of about 1 cm (½ an inch) between the stuffing and the tip of each courgette. Shake each courgette to loosen the filling.

TO COOK THE COURGETTES

3   Cover the base of a large pot with half the sliced tomatoes. Then add the stuffed courgettes in layers. Finally, cover the courgettes with the remaining sliced tomatoes.

4   Mix the boiling water with the tamarind paste. Then add the sieved tomatoes, salt, white pepper and cinnamon and mix the ingredients together.

5   Pour this mixture over the courgettes and sliced tomatoes. Cover the courgettes and tomatoes with a heavy heatproof plate to weigh them down, and then cover the pot with aluminium foil and a lid.

6   Allow to boil on a high heat, then reduce the heat to moderate and allow to simmer gently for 40–50 minutes, or until the courgettes are tender and the sauce slightly thickened.

Kousa mehshi

SERVES: **4**
PREPARATION TIME: **1 hour**
COOKING TIME: **1 hour**

FOR THE STUFFING
225 g (8 oz) lamb, coarsely minced

175 g (6 oz) risotto or pudding rice, soaked for 5 minutes in 570 ml (1 pint) hot water, then washed and drained

1 teaspoon ground allspice

1 teaspoon salt

½ teaspoon white pepper

1 teaspoon cinnamon

50 g (2 oz) pine nuts (optional)

75 ml (3 fl oz) corn oil

FOR THE COURGETTES
16 courgettes, washed and dried (about 1.4 kg/3 lb)

FOR THE SAUCE
6 tomatoes, sliced (for the base of the pot and to top the courgettes)

1.4 litres (2½ pints) boiling water

½ tablespoon tamarind paste

3 x 400 g (14 oz) tins chopped tomatoes, sieved

1 tablespoon salt

1 teaspoon white pepper

1 teaspoon cinnamon

1 teaspoon cornflour blended in 1 tablespoon cold water

TO GARNISH
½ teaspoon dried mint

YOU WILL ALSO NEED
a corer

TO SERVE

7 Serve the courgettes and tomatoes on a flat dish. Pass the sauce through a sieve to remove any tomato seeds, return to the saucepan and allow it to boil. Add the blended cornflour and water, and then the mint. Serve the sauce alongside the vegetables, and sprinkle the dried mint all over to produce the result in the picture.

TIPS

- A corer is essential for this recipe in order to achieve an even cavity for stuffing.

- Preparing the stuffing a little in advance enables the flavours to work together, so that the rice absorbs the meat juices and becomes less gluey.

- The courgettes can be cored in advance (for example the night before), washed, dried and placed in the refrigerator ready to be stuffed.

- Allowing the courgettes standing time with the sauce after cooking enhances their flavour.

Vegetarian stuffed courgettes

This vegetarian version of the previous recipe is a great favourite. Its ingredients are light yet full of flavour and once cooked it keeps for a long time. It is ideal for a dinner party with vegetarian friends. English courgettes can be used, but do try to get hold of the Middle Eastern variety as they are easier to core and prepare.

TO PREPARE THE STUFFING

1 In a large bowl, mix the rice with the salt, pepper, cinnamon, sugar and allspice. Add the tomatoes, parsley, onion, mint, garlic, pine nuts and corn or olive oil, mix well and set aside.

TO PREPARE THE COURGETTES

2 Core the courgettes, leaving one end intact to hold in the filling. Put the cored courgettes aside in the bowl of salted water. When they are all cored, rinse them under a running tap and drain. Then stuff them

---

a heavy heatproof plate

a large bowl containing salted water (about 1.7 litres (3 pints) and 3 tablespoons salt) in which to soak the courgettes after coring

Mehshi kousa soumi

SERVES: **4**
PREPARATION TIME: **1 hour**
COOKING TIME: **1 hour**

FOR THE STUFFING
150 g (5 oz) risotto or pudding rice, soaked for 5 minutes in 570 ml (1 pint) hot water, then washed and drained

1 teaspoon salt

½ teaspoon white pepper

½ teaspoon cinnamon

½ teaspoon sugar

½ teaspoon ground allspice

5 tomatoes, finely chopped

½ bunch flat leaf parsley, chopped

1 medium onion finely chopped

3 sprigs fresh mint leaves, finely chopped

2 cloves garlic, peeled and finely chopped

50 g (2 oz) pine nuts

75 ml (3 fl oz) corn oil or extra virgin olive oil

FOR THE COURGETTES

20 courgettes, washed and dried (about 1.75 kg/3¼ lb)

FOR THE SAUCE

4 tomatoes, sliced (for the base of the pot and to top the courgettes)

900 ml (1½ pints) boiling water

1 teaspoon tamarind paste

2 x 400 g (14 oz) tins chopped tomatoes, sieved

1 teaspoon salt

½ teaspoon white pepper

½ teaspoon cinnamon

YOU WILL ALSO NEED

a corer

a heavy heatproof plate

a large bowl containing salted water (about 1.7 litres (3 pints) and 3 tablespoons salt) in which to soak the courgettes after coring

with the vegetable stuffing, gently pushing the mixture into the cavity with your forefinger. Fill the courgettes all the way up as the filling once cooked will be reduced in volume.

TO COOK THE COURGETTES

3 Cover the base of a large pot with half the sliced tomatoes. Then add the stuffed courgettes in layers. Finally, cover the courgettes with the remaining sliced tomatoes.

4 Mix the boiling water with the tamarind paste. Then add the sieved tomatoes, salt, pepper and cinnamon and mix all the ingredients together.

5 Pour this mixture over the courgettes and sliced tomatoes in the pot. Cover the courgettes and tomatoes with a heavy heatproof plate to weigh them down. Cover the pot with aluminium foil and a lid. Allow to come to the boil on high heat, then reduce the heat and simmer gently on moderate heat for 40–50 minutes or until the courgettes are tender and the sauce thickened.

TO SERVE

6 Place the courgettes on a flat dish, cover with the tomato slices and serve the sauce on the side.

TIPS

- Do not core the courgettes too thinly as it is better to leave them thick so that they retain their texture and shape.

- The sauce does not need to be thickened as with the meat recipe as less water is used here.

- Simmer the courgettes on a low flame so as to cook the vegetables without crushing them to bits.

Stuffed baby courgettes

This is the third recipe in this chapter for stuffed courgettes. However, this time it's preferable to use baby courgettes because they look more attractive – see picture on next page. If you can't get hold of them easily, don't worry: you can use any size as long as they are firm.

TO PREPARE THE COURGETTES

1 Wash and core the courgettes, leaving one end intact to hold in the filling. Immerse the cored courgettes in the bowl of salty water and leave there for a minimum of 1 hour.

2 Drain and rinse the courgettes under a running tap. Pat dry with a cloth.

TO PREPARE THE STUFFING

3 Heat the olive oil in a frying pan. Then add the onions and sugar and stir on a high heat until light brown.

4 Add the meat and fry, stirring continuously to brown the meat.

5 Add the salt, pepper, cinnamon, allspice and nutmeg, lower the heat to moderate and cook for 5 more minutes stirring occasionally. Taste and adjust as necessary, then switch off the heat and set aside.

6 Add the pine nuts, parsley and sumac and allow to cool slightly.

TO STUFF AND FRY THE COURGETTES

7 Stuff the courgettes with the mixture, using your index finger to pack it gently into the cavity. Leave a small gap at one end.

8 Heat the vegetable oil in a frying pan, then shallow fry the courgettes until they are golden brown all over.

9 Drain the courgettes on absorbent kitchen paper.

TO PREPARE THE TOMATO SAUCE

10 Heat the oil, add the onion and sugar and sauté until slightly brown.

11 While stirring add the fresh tomatoes, the tinned tomatoes, water, salt, white pepper, cinnamon, allspice and butter and lower the heat to moderate. Allow the mixture to simmer for 5–10 minutes.

12 Add the pomegranate syrup and mix in thoroughly.

13 Add the cornflour mixture to thicken the sauce slightly. Allow to simmer for a minute, taste and adjust as necessary, then turn off the heat.

Ablama

SERVES: **4**
PREPARATION TIME: **1 hour**
COOKING TIME: **1 hour**

FOR THE COURGETTES
16 courgettes (about 1.4 kg/3 lb) – allow 4 small courgettes per person

110 ml (4 fl oz) vegetable oil for shallow frying

FOR THE STUFFING
75 ml (3 fl oz) extra virgin olive oil

1 onion, peeled and finely chopped

1 teaspoon sugar

225 g (8 oz) lamb, coarsely minced

1 teaspoon salt

½ teaspoon white pepper

½ teaspoon cinnamon

½ teaspoon ground allspice

½ teaspoon freshly grated nutmeg

25 g (1 oz) pine nuts

1 tablespoon chopped fresh parsley

½ teaspoon sumac (see p. 27)

FOR THE TOMATO SAUCE
25 ml (1 fl oz) extra virgin olive oil

1 onion, peeled and finely chopped

1 teaspoon granulated sugar

4 fresh tomatoes, skinned and finely chopped

400 g (14 oz) tin chopped tomatoes, sieved

100 ml (½ pint) boiling water

1 teaspoon salt

½ teaspoon white pepper

½ teaspoon cinnamon

TO COOK THE COURGETTES

14 Arrange the courgettes lengthways on a baking tray. Pour half the tomato sauce between the rows of courgettes and bake for 10–15 minutes. Reserve the rest of the sauce for later.

TO SERVE

15 Serve on a large warm plate with the reserved tomato sauce on one side and *Vermicelli rice* (see p. 167) to accompany.

16 The stuffed courgettes can also be served with a yoghurt sauce.

ALTERNATIVE VERSION WITH YOGHURT SAUCE

1 In a pan, blend together the yoghurt and water. Add the salt and pepper and heat gently, stirring until the liquid shows signs of boiling.

2 Add the cornflour mixture to thicken, stirring continuously. Simmer on a very low and gentle heat.

3 In a small frying pan, heat the ghee, add the fresh coriander and garlic and fry quickly.

4 Add this mixture to the yoghurt sauce, combine and set aside.

5 Cook the courgettes as before, replacing the tomato sauce with the yoghurt sauce.

6 Serve as before, but with the reserved yoghurt sauce drizzled over the top and with *White rice* (see p. 32) or *Vermicelli rice* (see p. 167) on the side.

TIPS

- Coring the courgettes can be done well in advance, a day before even. Core, wash and drain the courgettes and then put them in a bowl covered with cling film in the refrigerator.

- Everything can be prepared in advance, ready to be warmed and cooked through when required.

- Soaking the courgettes in salty water after coring improves the taste and reduces their absorbency of oil when being fried.

- The baking is just to combine the flavours, and you need only bake the dish lightly.

- If you bake the courgettes in a heatproof serving dish it can be served at the table straight from the oven.

½ teaspoon ground allspice

50 g (2 oz) unsalted butter

1 teaspoon pomegranate syrup

1 teaspoon cornflour blended in 25 ml (1 fl oz) cold water

FOR THE YOGHURT SAUCE (WHICH CAN BE USED AS AN ALTERNATIVE TO TOMATO)

900 ml (1½ pints) *Home-made yoghurt* (see p. 34)

300 ml (½ pint) water

1 teaspoon salt

½ teaspoon white pepper

1 tablespoon cornflour blended in 25 ml (1 fl oz) water

1 tablespoon ghee or clarified butter

1 tablespoon chopped fresh coriander

2 cloves garlic, peeled and finely chopped

TEMPERATURE
preheat the oven to gas mark 5, 375°F (190°C)

YOU WILL ALSO NEED
a corer

a baking tray

a large bowl containing salted water (1.2 litres (2 pints) and 2 tablespoons salt) in which to soak the courgettes after coring

TO ACCOMPANY
White rice (see p. 32)

Vermicelli rice (see p. 167)

SERVES: **4–5**

PREPARATION TIME: **1½ hours**

COOKING TIME: **1 hour**

FOR THE CABBAGE

3.4 litres (6 pints) boiling water

1 large cabbage or 2 small ones

FOR THE STUFFING

175 g (6 oz) risotto or pudding rice,
soaked for 5 minutes in 570 ml (1 pint)
hot water, then washed and drained

½ teaspoon saffron (optional)

225 g (8 oz) lamb, coarsely minced

1 teaspoon salt

½ teaspoon white pepper

½ teaspoon cinnamon

½ teaspoon ground allspice

½ teaspoon cumin

½ teaspoon freshly grated nutmeg

50 g (2 oz) pine nuts

½ teaspoon garlic, finely chopped

75 ml (3 fl oz) corn oil

TO COOK THE STUFFED CABBAGE

the reserved spines of cabbage leaves

1 teaspoon salt

½ teaspoon white pepper

2 tablespoons ghee or 50 ml
(2 fl oz) corn oil

1.2 litres (2 pints) boiling water

1 tablespoon vegetable ghee or
clarified butter

5 cloves garlic, peeled and finely
chopped or crushed

75 ml (3 fl oz) lemon juice

Stuffed cabbage

*Using the right variety of cabbage is the key to the simplicity of this dish.
Middle Eastern cabbages are large and therefore it is easy to separate the
leaves. It is a very therapeutic process, stuffing the leaves, and, of course,
there's the reward of a wonderful meal at the end.*

TO PREPARE THE CABBAGE

1 With a very sharp knife remove the core from the centre of the
cabbage as gently and carefully as possible.

2 Put the water into a pan and ensure that it is boiling vigorously.

3 Carefully place the cored cabbage into the pan of boiling water to
blanch. Weigh it down with the heavy plate to stop it floating in the
water and to speed up the blanching process.

4 Leave the cabbage to blanch for 10–12 minutes. Then turn the
cabbage to make sure the leaves have softened and have become
pliable enough to be removed easily. It's very important that you do
not overcook the cabbage. The cabbage should take about 20–25
minutes to blanch, depending upon the size and variety of cabbage.

5 Take the blanched cabbage out of the pan, and release the leaves
one by one using a knife. Remove the spine from each leaf. Arrange
the leaves in layers on a tray ready for stuffing. Do not discard the
spines; these will be used later.

TO PREPARE THE STUFFING

6 Meanwhile, transfer the drained rice into a bowl. Add the saffron (if
using) and mix in with the rice. Then add the minced lamb, salt, white
pepper, cinnamon, allspice, cumin, nutmeg, pine nuts, chopped garlic
and corn oil. Mix these ingredients together, then set aside.

TO STUFF THE CABBAGE

7 Take one leaf at a time and lay it flat on a chopping board.

8 Lay a small amount of stuffing (½–1 teaspoon, depending on the size
of the leaf) lengthways down the leaf. Fold the ends over the filling,
tuck them in, and roll the leaf around the stuffing to form a cigar shape.

9 Repeat the process with the rest of the leaves and stuffing.

TO COOK THE STUFFED CABBAGE

10 Place the spines previously removed from the cabbage leaves in the base of a pot.

11 Arrange the stuffed cabbage leaves in rows around the inside of the pot.

12 Season the cabbage leaves with salt and pepper, add the ghee or corn oil, and weigh the leaves down with a heavy heatproof plate.

13 Pour half the boiling water onto the cabbage leaves, cover with foil and/or lid and cook on a moderate heat for half an hour.

14 Add the rest of the boiling water.

15 Meanwhile, heat a small frying pan, add the vegetable ghee or clarified butter followed by the chopped garlic, sauté gently and then add to the cooking cabbage leaves in the pot.

16 Cook for a further 25–30 minutes, then add the lemon juice and taste the cabbage leaves to test whether they are tender and cooked. Switch off and set aside.

17 Allow the cooked cabbage leaves to stand for at least half an hour before serving.

18 Serve by turning the pot over onto a large platter with the juices all round the leaves, which gives it a glossy look and gives you the appetite to tuck in immediately. Sheer heaven!

TIPS

• The leaves should be tender and pliable but not overcooked after blanching.

• Prepare the stuffing while the leaves are being blanched.

YOU WILL ALSO NEED
a heavy heatproof plate

Stuffed potatoes

Mehshi batata

Not only is this a children's favourite, it's also popular with adults – it is therefore an essential standby! For best results, use fresh white potatoes that are all fairly similar in size.

SERVES: **4**

PREPARATION TIME: **50–60 minutes**

COOKING TIME: **40 minutes**

FOR THE POTATOES

12 good size white potatoes

a large bowl of salted water (approximately 2.3 litres (4 pints) and 2 large tablespoons of salt)

FOR THE STUFFING

2 tablespoons vegetable ghee or corn oil

1 onion, peeled and finely chopped

1 teaspoon granulated sugar

225 g (8 oz) lamb, coarsely minced

½ teaspoon ground allspice

½ teaspoon cinnamon

1 teaspoon salt

½ teaspoon white pepper

½ teaspoon freshly grated nutmeg

50 g (2 oz) pine nuts

1 tablespoon chopped fresh parsley

FOR THE SAUCE

50 ml (2 fl oz) extra virgin olive oil

1 onion, peeled and thinly sliced

1 teaspoon granulated sugar

8 salad tomatoes or 4 beef tomatoes, skinned and finely chopped

225 g (8 oz) tin chopped tomatoes, sieved

275 ml (½ pint) boiling water

1 teaspoon salt

½ teaspoon ground allspice

½ teaspoon cinnamon

½ teaspoon white pepper

TO PREPARE THE POTATOES

1 Peel and core potatoes and soak in salted water while making the stuffing.

2 Drain the potatoes and dry on absorbent kitchen paper.

3 Heat the deep-fat fryer to 375°F (190°C) and fry the potatoes until slightly browned. Drain on kitchen paper.

TO PREPARE THE STUFFING

4 Heat the ghee or corn oil in a frying pan. Add the onion and sugar and sauté together until the onion is slightly brown.

5 Add the minced lamb, and cook on a high heat with the onions until the meat has browned.

6 Add the allspice, cinnamon, salt, pepper and nutmeg. Mix together thoroughly and fry on a high heat, stirring continuously. *

7 Lower the heat and allow the mixture to cook together for 5 minutes, stirring occasionally. Taste and adjust accordingly and switch off the heat.

8 Add pine nuts and parsley, mix in and set aside.

TO PREPARE THE SAUCE

9 Heat the olive oil in a deep frying pan. Add the sliced onion and sugar and sauté the onion until it is soft and slightly brown.

10 Add the fresh tomatoes, tinned tomatoes, water, salt, allspice, cinnamon, pepper, nutmeg and butter and allow to simmer gently on a moderate heat for 10 minutes, stirring occasionally.

11 Add the pomegranate syrup and cook for 5 more minutes.

12 Take off the heat, taste and adjust accordingly.

TO ASSEMBLE AND COOK

13 Stuff the cavity in the fried potatoes with the mince filling.

Simply Lebanese

½ teaspoon freshly grated nutmeg

50 g (2 oz) unsalted butter

1 tablespoon pomegranate syrup
(see p. 26)

(see p. 26)

TEMPERATURE
preheat the oven to gas mark 5,
375°F (190°C)

YOU WILL ALSO NEED
a corer

a deep-fat fryer

a heatproof serving dish or
a baking tray

TO ACCOMPANY
Cucumber and yoghurt salad
(see pp. 34–5)

(see pp. 34–5)

Mehshi jazzar

SERVES: 4
PREPARATION TIME: 1 hour
COOKING TIME: 1 hour

FOR THE STUFFING
175 g (6 oz) risotto or pudding rice,
soaked for 5 minutes in 570 ml
(1 pint) hot water, then washed
and drained

½ teaspoon saffron (optional)

225 g (8 oz) lamb, coarsely minced

½ teaspoon ground allspice

½ teaspoon freshly grated nutmeg

½ teaspoon cinnamon

14 Arrange the potatoes in a heatproof dish or on a baking tray and pour the half the tomato sauce in between the rows of potatoes, reserving the other half for later.

15 Bake in the oven for 10–12 minutes.

TO SERVE

16 Serve with the rest of the sauce on one side with *Cucumber and yoghurt salad*, or one of the other salads in the book.

TIPS

• Dry the potatoes before frying – this helps to stop them spitting when they are added to the oil.

• The potatoes can be cored in advance and kept in salty water.

Stuffed carrots

For this dish the carrots are cooked in a most unusual way, which ensures the flavours are beautifully infused. The sauce creates a unique sweet and sour combination, which will grow on you the more you eat it. As for the carrots – choose ones that are similar in size. A good corer makes the job easier, so look for one with sharp edges. Coring the carrots is the only difficult part in this recipe, but this is where family solidarity comes into play and the husband or partner can step in to help!

TO PREPARE THE STUFFING

1 Transfer the clean rice to a bowl. Mix in the saffron (if using), followed by the mince, allspice, nutmeg, cinnamon, salt, pepper and corn oil, and put to one side.

1 teaspoon salt

½ teaspoon white pepper

75 ml (3 fl oz) corn oil

FOR THE CARROTS

16 evenly sized carrots

a large bowl containing salted water 2.3 litres (4 pints) and 2 large tablespoons of salt

110 ml (4 fl oz) olive oil or corn oil

2 x 400 g (14 oz) tins chopped tomatoes, sieved

1 teaspoon tamarind paste blended in 275 ml (½ pint) boiling water

1 teaspoon salt

½ teaspoon white pepper

½ teaspoon cinnamon

YOU WILL ALSO NEED

a corer

TO ACCOMPANY

Fattoush (see p. 69)

Tabbouleh (see pp. 70–1)

TO PREPARE THE CARROTS

2 Peel and core the carrots leaving the thinnest end closed to hold the filling. Transfer to the bowl of salty water while you core the rest of the carrots. Reserve the centres of the carrots for use later.

3 Wash and drain the carrots.

4 Fill the carrots with the stuffing, leaving ½ cm (¼ inch) space at the top.

TO COOK

5 Shallow fry the stuffed carrots in the olive or corn oil until caramel all over in colour.

6 Meanwhile, mix the tinned tomatoes with the tamarind and water mixture and set aside.

7 Put the reserved centres of the cored carrots in the base of a pot. Add the fried carrots, the salt, white pepper and cinnamon.

8 Pour the tomato mixture on top of the carrots.

9 Cover with aluminium foil and/or a lid, and allow to cook on a moderate heat for 30–40 minutes until the carrots are tender and the rice cooked.

TO SERVE

10 Place the cooked, stuffed carrots on a flat plate and serve with the tomato sauce on one side. Serve with a *Fattoush* salad and/or *Tabbouleh*.

TIPS

• Do not over-stuff the carrots. This will allow the rice to cook more evenly.

• The sauce has a tendency to thicken, so add water if you need to thin it.

• The reserved carrot centres add a sweetness to the dish, and can be served separately along side the fried, stuffed carrots if you prefer.

Okra stew

Okra, or bamya as it is known in Arabic, has its own distinctive flavour and texture. You either love it or hate it. That said, it's very popular and much in demand, especially within the Gulf States as a great accompaniment to their rice dishes. Okra is generally available fresh in supermarkets. Look out particularly for the smaller variety, which is tastier and milder in flavour than the normal-size okra. Frozen okra is widely available and is of great quality, if not better quality than the fresh. Don't hesitate in using it – you can fry it from frozen, but be careful not to over-brown it.

TO PREPARE THE MEAT

1 Heat a pot and add the olive oil followed by the meat pieces. On a high heat sauté the meat for about 3 minutes until the pieces are light brown.

2 Add the peppercorns, cardamom, allspice pods, onion, lemon slice and salt. Pour in the water, allow it to come to the boil and then reduce the heat to moderate.

3 Cover the pot, and allow contents to simmer gently for 40–50 minutes, checking regularly. The meat should be cooked through and tender.

4 Switch off the heat, drain the meat pieces and reserve the juices in a jug.

TO PREPARE THE TOMATO SAUCE

5 Heat a pan. Add the olive oil followed by the onion and sugar and sauté on a high heat until light brown.

6 Lower the heat to moderate, add the garlic and chopped fresh coriander and stir to mix.

7 Add the chopped fresh tomatoes, salt, pepper, cinnamon, ground allspice, ground coriander and the reserved stock from cooking the meat, butter, pomegranate syrup (if used) and allow everything to cook together for 10 minutes on a moderate heat.

8 Add the sieved tomatoes and continue to cook for another 7 minutes, simmering moderately.

9 Taste and adjust accordingly, add the reserved meat pieces, cook together for a few minutes, then switch off and set aside.

Bamya

SERVES: **4**
PREPARATION TIME: **20 minutes**
COOKING TIME: **1 hour**

FOR THE MEAT

50 ml (2 fl oz) extra virgin olive oil

1 boneless shoulder lamb with fat removed, chopped into fairly small pieces

4 whole peppercorns

2 whole cardamom pods

2 whole allspice pods (if available)

½ onion, peeled

1 lemon slice

1 teaspoon salt

2.3 litres (4 pints) boiling water

FOR THE TOMATO SAUCE

2 tablespoons extra virgin olive oil

1 medium onion, peeled and finely chopped

½ teaspoon granulated sugar

4 cloves garlic, peeled and very finely chopped or crushed

½ bunch fresh coriander leaves, finely chopped

6 tomatoes, skinned and finely chopped

1 teaspoon salt

½ teaspoon white pepper

½ teaspoon cinnamon

½ teaspoon ground allspice

1 teaspoon ground coriander

275 ml (½ pint) reserved meat stock

75 g (3 oz) unsalted butter

400 g (14 oz) tin chopped tomatoes, sieved

1 tablespoon pomegranate syrup
(optional) (see p. 26)

FOR THE OKRA
350 g (12 oz) fresh or frozen okra

YOU WILL ALSO NEED
a deep-fat fryer

TO PREPARE THE OKRA

10 Meanwhile, fry the okra in the preheated deep-fat fryer at 375°F (190°C) until it is light in colour and cooked through. This will take just a few minutes. Drain on absorbent kitchen paper.

TO ASSEMBLE AND SERVE

11 Add the fried okra to the tomato and meat sauce and heat through for a few minutes.

12 Serve with *Vermicelli rice* (see p. 167).

TIPS

• This stew can easily be adapted to suit vegetarians: replace the meat stock with boiling water, and omit the lamb pieces altogether.

• The temperature of the oil in the fryer should be as stated, so that the okra fries and browns quickly when immersed in the oil rather than stewing.

• The okra only needs to be light brown in colour as it will be cooked further with the tomato and meat sauce.

Mousakhan

SERVES: 4
PREPARATION TIME: **40 minutes**
COOKING TIME: **50 minutes**

FOR THE POUSSINS OR CHICKEN
1 teaspoon salt

½ teaspoon white pepper

1 teaspoon sumac (see p. 27)

1 tablespoon lemon juice

2 tablespoons extra virgin olive oil

2 poussins, washed, dried and cut into 8 pieces – 4 pieces of breast, 4 legs, or 8 chicken thigh portions

Chicken in Halabi bread

Translated into English, mousakhan *means 'cooked and heated'. This is one of the best ways I know to cook poussins, and the spicy caramelised onions ensure that the final dish has a distinctive taste, despite using simple ingredients. Not only that, the bread stays succulent and moist but with a crunchy crust. If you don't believe me, just try it!*

1 Mix the salt, pepper, sumac, lemon juice and olive oil and use to marinade the poussins or chicken. Cover with cling film and chill in the refrigerator for a minimum of half an hour.

2 Meanwhile, heat the 175 ml (6 fl oz) extra virgin olive oil in a deep frying pan. When it is hot, add the sliced onions, sugar, sumac and pepper. Mix together with the onions for 2–3 more minutes.

FOR THE ONIONS

110 ml (4 fl oz) extra virgin olive oil

3 red onions, peeled and finely sliced

1 teaspoon sugar

1 tablespoon sumac (see p. 27)

½ teaspoon white pepper

4 *Halabi* (bread wraps, see pp. 212–13)

1 teaspoon pine nuts, toasted

YOU WILL ALSO NEED

a griddle pan (if you have one)

a baking tray

TO ACCOMPANY

Cucumber and yoghurt salad (see pp. 34–5), mixed salad, or *Aubergine mousakaa* (see pp. 87–8)

3 Heat the griddle pan to very hot and add the marinaded poussin pieces. Grill for 2 minutes on each side to brown and then transfer the pan to under the oven grill. Grill for 10 minutes on the highest setting, turning the poussins once halfway. If you do not have a griddle pan, simply place under the grill for a couple of minutes longer.

4 Take 1 *Halabi bread* wrap and lay it flat on a board. Pile pieces of poussin (1 leg, 1 breast) on top along with 2 tablespoons of the onion mixture and a few pine nuts, then fold the four corners of the bread to form a square parcel.

5 Brush the parcel all over with some oil from the pan in which you cooked the onions. You now have one completed *Mousakhan*, which you should place on a baking tray.

6 Repeat this process with your remaining poussin pieces, onion mix and *Halabi*.

7 Grill the *Mousakhans* for 2 minutes each, turning over halfway through to brown both sides.

8 Serve with *Mousakaa* and any salad of your choice from the *mezze* selection. I particularly recommend the *Cucumber and yoghurt salad*.

TIPS

- If you do not have the time or the inclination to make the *Halabi* yourself, these days you can easily buy bread wraps which will work just as well from most supermarkets.

- Make sure the bread is baked until light golden brown and a bit crispy at the corners.

- If you don't have a griddle, use a heavy frying pan that can withstand the heat from the oven grill.

Baked kibbeh

In Arabic cooking, bisineyeh *means 'in a tray'. My version of* kibbeh *is a 'lazy' version, but doesn't lose any of its flavour. The dish is excellent for any occasion, be it a dinner party, family meal or even a picnic. And it retains its goodness, even at room temperature.*

1 Take the cooled filling and stir in the parsley.

2 Grease the baking tray with half the amount of ghee.

3 Divide the *kibbeh* mixture into two. Take the first half and sandwich it between the two polythene bags to create a sheet. Repeat with the second half of mixture.

4 Transfer the first sheet of *kibbeh* carefully to a greased tray, discarding the polythene bags.

5 Spread the filling neatly and evenly over the sheet of *kibbeh*.

6 Put the second sheet of *kibbeh* carefully on top of the filling, and tidy the edges neatly.

7 With a sharp knife, divide the *kibbeh* into pieces to make it easier to segment later.

8 Brush the top of the *kibbeh* with the 2 tablespoons of ghee or butter.

9 Place the tray in your hot oven for 15 minutes, checking it after this period.

10 Take out and serve with *Aubergine mousakaa* (see pp. 87–8) or *Fattoush* (see p. 69).

TIPS

- The *Kibbeh bisineyeh* can be prepared well in advance up to the baking stage, to be baked when needed.

- The *Kibbeh bisineyeh* freezes well: freeze it before the baking stage, to be defrosted gradually in the refrigerator and baked when needed.

- When brushing the ghee on the top layer of *kibbeh*, make sure the ghee goes through the partition of the slices as this ensures a moist *Kibbeh bisineyeh*.

Kibbeh bisineyeh

SERVES: **4**
PREPARATION TIME: **15 minutes**
COOKING TIME: **15 minutes**

FOR THE KIBBEH SHELL
as for *Kibbeh makleih* (see pp. 112–13, steps 1–2 inclusive)

2 tablespoons ghee or clarified butter

FOR THE FILLING
as for *Kibbeh makleih* (see pp. 112–13, steps 3–6 inclusive)

2 tablespoons chopped fresh parsley

TEMPERATURE
preheat the oven to gas mark 7, 425°F (220°C)

YOU WILL ALSO NEED
a non-stick baking tray 15 x 20.5 cm (6 x 8 inches)

two large polythene bags

Deek roumi

SERVES: 6 generously

PREPARATION TIME: 30 minutes, plus overnight marination of the turkey

COOKING TIME: 2¼ hours

FOR THE TURKEY
1 fresh turkey 1.8 kg–2.3 kg (4 lb–5 lb) in weight, with giblets

75 g (3 oz) butter for basting

FOR THE MARINADE
1 teaspoon white pepper

1 teaspoon freshly ground black pepper

1 teaspoon freshly grated nutmeg

½ teaspoon cinnamon

1 teaspoon ground cardamom

1 tablespoon salt

1 tablespoon honey

110 ml (4 fl oz) freshly squeezed lemon juice, reserving the squeezed lemon halves

110 ml (4 fl oz) corn oil

FOR THE STOCK
giblets from the turkey

1.75 litres (3 pints) water

½ teaspoon salt

1 medium onion

1 carrot

4 whole cardamom pods

4 whole black peppercorns

½ lemon

FOR THE STUFFING
50 ml (2 fl oz) extra virgin olive oil

50 g (2 oz) unsalted butter

1 bunch spring onions, chopped

2 cloves garlic, peeled and finely chopped

My turkey

For a long time I followed my mother's recipe and always stuffed my turkey the traditional way with rice and meat, not realising that it did not do the turkey meat enough justice. After enjoying a Christmas meal at a friend's house, I was converted to her way of cooking turkey. Ever since then, this dish has become the most sought after meal in our house. That is why I have decided to share the recipe with you. Turkey is great if it is cooked in a way that enhances its natural flavours by keeping the recipe simple and the meat moist. If the meat is dry it kills the flavour, so this is the most important thing to avoid. Turkey is of low calorific value too, which is another bonus. Fresh turkey is preferable to frozen, as this improves the end result. If using frozen, defrost thoroughly and follow the recipe as you would for fresh turkey.

TO MAKE THE MARINADE
1 Mix together all the ingredients in a food processor or just in a bowl.

TO PREPARE THE TURKEY
2 Wash and dry the turkey. Remove the giblets and put them to one side.

3 Rub the butter under the skin of the meat under the turkey wings.

4 Rub the cavity and the whole turkey with the marinade. Put the squeezed lemon halves inside the cavity.

5 Place the turkey in a large dish, cover with the rest of the marinade and chill in the refrigerator covered with cling film for at least 4 hours, preferably overnight.

TO MAKE STOCK FOR THE GRAVY
6 Clean the giblets and put in a pan with 1.75 litres (3 pints) of cold water, together with the salt, onion, carrot, cardamom, peppercorns and lemon.

7 Cover the pan, and allow ingredients to simmer gently for 40–50 minutes to form stock for the gravy. Once ready, strain the stock and put to one side until required.

TO MAKE THE STUFFING
8 Heat a deep frying pan. Add the olive oil and butter, followed by the spring onions, chopped ginger and garlic. Sauté together for a few minutes.

9 Add the mushrooms and lemon juice and stir the mixture.

10 Add the salt, white pepper, black pepper, ground cardamom and cinnamon, followed by the chopped figs and stir.

11 Lastly add the chopped parsley, sage, thyme, pine nuts and breadcrumbs and mix together. Set aside.

TO COOK THE TURKEY

12 Remove the turkey from the marinade.

13 Fill the main cavity and neck cavity with the stuffing. Secure both cavities with toothpicks or string.

14 Place the turkey face down on the large oven tray and cover with a double layer of aluminium foil. Place in your hot oven for 1 hour.

15 Now turn the turkey on to its back and cook, covered, for a further 50 minutes, basting it regularly.

16 Remove the aluminium foil to allow the bird to brown. Cook for a further 10–15 minutes. Put the grill on for the last few minutes if necessary.

17 Take the turkey out of the oven and allow to stand for about 30 minutes while you make the gravy.

TO MAKE THE GRAVY

18 Heat a pan and add the butter. When melted add the mushrooms and sauté for a few minutes, stirring continuously.

19 Add the lemon juice, salt and reserved giblet stock.

20 Allow it to come to the boil, then add the cornflour mixture and stir in. Allow to simmer for 1 minute.

21 Fold the double cream into the gravy and allow to bubble. It is now ready for serving.

TO SERVE

22 Carve the turkey and arrange on a platter. Drizzle the gorgeous gravy on to the slices of turkey and serve the rest on the side, along with boiled potatoes and other vegetables. Merry Christmas!

2–3 cm (¾–1¼ inch) root ginger, peeled and chopped

110 g (4 oz) white button mushrooms, halved

25 ml (1 fl oz) lemon juice

1 teaspoon salt

½ teaspoon white pepper

½ teaspoon freshly ground black pepper (optional)

½ teaspoon ground cardamom

½ teaspoon cinnamon

110 g (4 oz) dried figs

1 tablespoon chopped fresh parsley

1 tablespoon chopped fresh or ½ tablespoon dried sage

1 tablespoon chopped fresh or ½ tablespoon dried thyme

50 g (2 oz) pine nuts

110 g (4 oz) breadcrumbs

FOR THE GRAVY
50 g (2 oz) unsalted butter

225 g (8 oz) button mushrooms

1 tablespoon lemon juice

¼ teaspoon salt

stock (see above)

1 teaspoon cornflour blended in 25 ml (1 fl oz) cold water

50 ml (2 fl oz) double cream

TEMPERATURE
preheat the oven to gas mark 7, 425°F (220°C)

YOU WILL ALSO NEED
an oven tray covered with aluminium foil

FISH

Depending on what type you choose, fish can be robust or delicate; it can be cooked almost instantly or infused with flavours over a longer period of time; it can be complex or it can be simple; it can be an ideal dish for a special occasion, or it can be a simple meal. And despite the small number of Lebanese fish dishes in this chapter, they seem to cover all the points I mention – which makes them very special indeed.

Sea bass with chilli sauce

Here we have a sturdy fish that you can serve with a contrast of flavours either by preparing it with chilli or tahini sauce. The chilli sauce is very light, and the tahini sauce a bit more rich and traditionally Lebanese. Take your pick, or try both!

SERVES: 4

PREPARATION TIME: 40 minutes, plus at least 1 hour for marinating the fish

COOKING TIME: 40 minutes

FOR THE FISH

900 g (2 lb) sea bass, cleaned and scaled with fins and gills removed

1 lemon, sliced

2 teaspoons salt

½ teaspoon white pepper

75 g (2 oz) butter

1 clove garlic, peeled and sliced

2 tablespoons extra virgin olive oil

½ teaspoon freshly ground black pepper

FOR THE CHILLI SAUCE

3 tablespoons extra virgin olive oil

1 medium onion, peeled and finely chopped

½ teaspoon granulated sugar

2 cloves garlic, peeled and finely chopped

½ red chilli, deseeded and finely chopped

2 cm (1¼ inch) root ginger, peeled and finely chopped (optional)

1 tablespoon chopped fresh coriander

1 tablespoon chopped fresh parsley

½ teaspoon ground allspice

½ teaspoon cinnamon

1 teaspoon salt

75 ml (3 fl oz) water

6 tomatoes, skinned and finely chopped

TO PREPARE THE FISH FOR MARINATING

1 Wash and dry the fish, and rub all over with half the lemon slices and half the salt. Place the fish on double sheets of foil.

2 Mix the rest of the salt and the white pepper together and rub all over the fish. Stuff the inside with the butter, garlic and some of the lemon slices.

3 Top the fish with the remaining lemon slices, drizzle generously with the oil and sprinkle all over with the freshly ground black pepper.

4 Wrap the foil around the fish by scrunching it or folding it neatly over and chill for at least 1 hour.

TO PREPARE THE CHILLI SAUCE

5 In a frying pan, heat the olive oil. Then add the onion and sugar and sauté well until the onions are light brown.

6 Add the garlic, chilli, ginger (if using), fresh coriander, parsley, allspice, cinnamon, salt, water and chopped fresh tomatoes. Allow to cook for 5 minutes on a moderate heat.

7 Add the tinned tomatoes and their juice, Tabasco, lemon juice and pomegranate syrup. Allow to cook for 5 more minutes. Set aside after adjusting to taste.

ALTERNATIVELY, TO PREPARE THE TAHINI SAUCE

- In a frying pan, heat the olive oil, add the onions, garlic and sugar and sauté together until the onion is light brown.

- Then add the green chilli, parsley, fresh and ground coriander, cumin, half the salt and white pepper. Allow to cook together on a medium heat for 1 minute.

- Meanwhile, mix the tahini with 220 ml (8 fl oz) of the water and blend together well. Then add the lemon juice, the rest of the salt and lastly the rest of the water, mixing well.

. 400 g (14 oz) tin chopped
tomatoes, sieved

1 tablespoon Tabasco

1 tablespoon lemon juice

½ tablespoon pomegranate syrup
(see p. 26)

FOR THE TAHINI SAUCE

3 tablespoons extra virgin olive oil

1 onion, peeled and finely sliced

2 cloves garlic, peeled and finely
chopped

1 teaspoon granulated sugar

½ green chilli, deseeded and finely
chopped

1 tablespoon chopped fresh parsley

2 tablespoons chopped fresh coriander

½ teaspoon ground coriander

½ teaspoon cumin

2 teaspoons salt

½ teaspoon white pepper

220 ml (8 fl oz) tahini

295 ml (11 fl oz) water

150 ml (5 fl oz) lemon juice

1 teaspoon Dijon mustard

TO GARNISH

pine nuts

sprigs of fresh parsley

lemon slices

TEMPERATURE

preheat the oven to gas mark 7,
425°F (220°C)

- Add the tahini to the frying mixture. Allow to simmer for a few minutes, then add the mustard. Adjust the seasoning to taste and set aside.

TO COOK THE FISH

8 Put the wrapped fish on a baking tray and bake for 20–25 minutes.

TO SERVE

9 Lay the fish on a large plate and peel off the skin gently and carefully. Pour whichever sauce you have prepared over the top. Scatter with pine nuts and garnish with fresh parsley, arranging the lemon slices at the side, and serve with *Lebanese caesar salad* (pp. 72–3) and *Chilli potatoes* (p. 89) or *White rice* (see p. 32).

TIPS

- It is better to have one large fish for this recipe rather than two small ones, as you will get better flavour.

- Test the sea bass before taking out of the oven; it should be cooked yet firm.

- The sea bass, once covered with the sauce, can be put under the oven grill for few minutes to bake lightly.

- For a more chilli sauce, add 1 tablespoon of the *Red chilli sauce* as described on pp. 38–9.

- In the tahini sauce, the amount of chopped chilli is optional – it can be omitted altogether.

- The tahini sauce should be smooth but not too thick – if it becomes too thick do not hesitate to add more water.

- The sauces can be served on the side rather than poured over the fish as suggested.

Sayadiyeh

This dish is the pride of Lebanese cuisine. The idea was originally imported, but Lebanese details and enhancements were added to it – hence the combination of flavours and contrasts which make it a challenge to make and master. The rice is by no means simple, but if you follow the instructions attentively you will manage. Cod is the best fish for this recipe because its texture withstands the handling required and it also absorbs the full range of influences from the special rice and tahini sauce. Before you start cooking, read the recipe through carefully to get an idea of the procedure. The order of cooking: a) prepare the brown sauce; b) cook the rice; c) bake the fish; d) prepare the garnish; e) prepare the tahini sauce; f) assemble the dish and serve. Enjoy!

TO PREPARE THE BASE FOR BROWN SAUCE AND STOCK FOR THE RICE

1 Heat a frying pan. Add the olive oil, followed by the onions and brown sugar, and allow to caramelise on a high heat until the mixture is a deep-brown colour.

2 Meanwhile, to a medium-sized pot add the boiling water, cardamom, cumin, cinnamon, saffron, allspice, coriander, salt, pepper, pomegranate syrup, tamarind paste, Tabasco, lemon juice and mustard. Allow this liquid to simmer for 10 minutes to infuse the flavours.

3 Add the caramelised onions to the liquid, and leave to simmer for a further 10 minutes.

4 Sieve the liquid through a sieve or a mouli, making sure that all the onion pulp is pushed through. This mixture forms the base for the brown sauce and the stock for cooking the rice.

TO COOK THE RICE

5 Heat a pan, then add the vegetable ghee or corn oil. Once hot add the drained rice, mix into the oil and heat through while stirring.

6 In a separate, ovenproof pan, bring 700 ml (1¼ pints) of the brown stock to boiling point, then pour into the rice. Mix once, allow to cook without a lid for a couple of minutes, then put on a lid and put the pan into the preheated oven for 10–12 minutes.

7 The rice is ready once all the water has been absorbed and you can see a few holes in the rice. Then remove from the oven and set aside.

SERVES: **4**

PREPARATION TIME: **1 hour**

COOKING TIME: **50 minutes**

FOR THE BROWN SAUCE

75 ml (3 fl oz) extra virgin olive oil

2 large onions, peeled and thinly sliced

1 tablespoon brown sugar

2.3 litres (4 pints) boiling water

½ teaspoon ground cardamom

½ teaspoon cumin

½ teaspoon cinnamon

1 teaspoon saffron

½ teaspoon ground allspice

½ teaspoon ground coriander

1 teaspoon salt

½ teaspoon white pepper

1 tablespoon pomegranate syrup (see p. 26)

1 tablespoon tamarind paste (see pp. 27–8)

1 teaspoon Tabasco

25 ml (1 fl oz) lemon juice

1 teaspoon Dijon mustard

1 level tablespoon cornflour blended in 25 ml (1 fl oz) water

FOR THE RICE

50 g (2 oz) vegetable ghee or 50 ml (2 fl oz) corn oil

450 g (1 lb) basmati rice, soaked in 570 ml (1 pint) boiling water for 5 minutes, then drained, rinsed under hot running water, then drained again in a colander

TO COMPLETE THE BROWN SAUCE

8 Heat the remaining stock to the boil. Thicken with the cornflour mixture and allow to simmer for a few minutes. The sauce is then ready for serving.

TO COOK THE FISH

9 Place the cod fillets on an oven tray. Mix the salt, pepper, olive oil and lemon juice together and pour over the fillets.

10 Dot the fillets with the butter, cover with foil and place in the oven for 12–15 minutes. Take out and keep warm until you are ready to serve.

TO PREPARE THE GARNISH

11 Fry the onion in a little olive oil until crisp and dark brown in colour. Drain on absorbent kitchen paper and set aside.

TO PREPARE THE TAHINI SAUCE

12 Heat a pan, add the olive oil, onions and sugar and fry quickly together.

13 Mix in the garlic, salt, cumin, ground coriander, pepper and ground coriander and fry on a low heat for a couple of minutes.

14 Blend the tahini with half the water, then add the lemon juice followed by the rest of the water, stirring carefully to end up with a smooth sauce.

15 Pour the tahini sauce on to the frying mixture, stirring continuously. Adjust seasoning to taste, and the sauce is ready.

TO SERVE

16 In a deep-sided dish, layer the crisp fried onions on the base, and scatter on the pine nuts.

17 Cover this base with layers of cooked cod and drizzle with the cod's own juices from roasting. Top with the cooked rice. Tidy the sides of the mixture and press down gently.

18 Turn the deep-sided dish and its contents upside down on to a larger serving dish.

19 Serve the brown sauce and tahini sauce, which should preferably be warm, on the side.

FOR THE FISH
900 g (2 lb) cod fillets, skinned and cut into large pieces

1 teaspoon salt

1 teaspoon white pepper

50 ml (2 fl oz) extra virgin olive oil

50 ml (2 fl oz) lemon juice

50 g (2 oz) unsalted butter, diced

FOR THE TAHINI SAUCE
75 ml (3 fl oz) extra virgin olive oil

2 onions, peeled and thinly sliced

1 teaspoon granulated sugar

1 clove garlic, peeled and finely chopped

1 teaspoon salt

½ teaspoon cumin

½ teaspoon white pepper

½ teaspoon ground coriander

220 ml (8 fl oz) tahini

295 ml (11 fl oz) water

150 ml (5 fl oz) lemon juice

TO GARNISH
2 large onions, peeled and thinly sliced

50 g (2 oz) pine nuts

TEMPERATURE
preheat the oven to gas mark 4, 350°F (180°C)

YOU WILL ALSO NEED
a deep-sided rectangular dish

TIPS

- Everything that is prepared can be set aside and reheated as this recipe is cooking in stages. The serving dish should be heated in the oven.

- The traditional way to eat the dish is to have both sauces on your plate at once to provide a contrast of flavours.

- A simple salad should be the only accompaniment to this dish as it is quite rich and you do not want to interfere too much with it.

Samak bi warak inab

SERVES: **4**

PREPARATION TIME: **15 minutes**

COOKING TIME: **20 minutes**

1 teaspoon salt

½ teaspoon white pepper

½ teaspoon cumin

75 ml (3 fl oz) lemon juice

50 ml (2 fl oz) extra virgin olive oil

700 g (1½ lb) cod fillets skinned and cut into 4 portions

110 g (4 oz) vine leaves (see p. 49)

50 g (2 oz) butter, cut into four portions

TEMPERATURE
preheat the oven to gas mark 6, 400°F (200°C)

YOU WILL ALSO NEED
a baking tray lined with aluminium foil

Cod wrapped in vine leaves

This recipe was created by accident, after I had some vine leaves left over from another recipe and some cod in my freezer. I decided to put the two together and the result was truly exotic.

1 Mix the salt, pepper, cumin, lemon juice and olive oil together and rub the pieces of cod all over with the mixture. Leave the cod in the marinade while preparing the vine leaves. (See p. 49 for method.)

2 Lay two vine leaves on a plate. Place a piece of cod onto one vine leaf and fold the other one over to wrap the cod.

3 Repeat with the rest of the pieces of cod and place them on the baking tray. Dot each piece with butter and place in the oven for 12 minutes.

4 Remove and serve with either *Loubieh bizeit* (see p. 88) or *Mousakaa* (see pp. 87–8), and *Fattoush* (see p. 69) or any Lebanese salad of your choice.

TIPS

- If frozen fish is used, make sure you defrost it thoroughly before using.

- Fresh vine leaves can be used but blanch them first in boiling water as you would with the pickled variety.

- If the vine leaves are small use more than two leaves to wrap the cod.

- The wraps can be prepared well in advance and kept chilled in the refrigerator until you are ready to bake them. A great dinner party dish.

Prawn stew

This recipe was originally used for cooking chicken in our house, but on an occasion when I had prawns instead, I decided to use this method and the result was just as good if not better. The only thing that had to be altered was the time of cooking as prawns obviously do not need as long as chicken. The children loved it, hence this recipe is a good way to introduce them to prawns at an early stage.

TO COOK THE PRAWNS

1 In a large pan melt the butter, add the onion and leek and sauté to slightly soften them. Add the garlic slices, mix thoroughly and then add the prawns. Stir well and as soon as the prawns start to change colour add the tomato purée, mixing it in thoroughly.

2 Add the tomatoes, salt, pepper, cinnamon, allspice, tamarind paste (if using) and lemon juice and stir to mix thoroughly.

3 Add the water and allow to boil, then simmer. Remove the prawns from the stock 7 minutes after it has boiled and set aside to cool. Leave the stock to cook gently for a few minutes to enhance the flavours and to thicken slightly.

4 Peel the prawns and remove the black vein at the back of every prawn using a sharp knife. Keep covered once all the prawns have been peeled.

5 Strain the cooking stock through a sieve, return to the pan and allow to simmer gently on low flame.

TO COOK THE RICE

6 Heat the butter in a pan. Add the rice, stir in the salt and then pour in 700 ml (1 ¼) pints of the cooking stock, mix once, lower the heat, cover and leave the rice to simmer for 1 minute to absorb some of the liquid.

7 Transfer thereafter to the heated oven and leave to finish cooking for a further 5–7 minutes. Take out and set aside until ready to serve.

TO MAKE THE SAUCE

8 Add the Dijon mustard and Tabasco (if using) to the simmering stock and mix well. Blend the cornflour and the water together and add to the sauce, stirring continuously.

Yakhnet kreides

SERVES: **4–5**
PREPARATION TIME: **30 minutes**
COOKING TIME: **30 minutes**

FOR THE PRAWNS
75 g (3 oz) unsalted butter

1 large onion, peeled and finely chopped

1 leek, finely sliced

2 cloves garlic, peeled and sliced

1 kg (2.2 lb) large fresh king prawns with their shells, washed

50 g (2 oz) tomato purée

250 g (9 oz) tomatoes, finely chopped

1 teaspoon salt

½ teaspoon white pepper

½ teaspoon cinnamon

½ teaspoon ground allspice

1 tablespoon tamarind paste (optional)

25 ml (1 fl oz) lemon juice

1 litre (1¾ pints) water

FOR THE RICE
50 g (2 oz) unsalted butter

450 g (1 lb) basmati rice soaked in 570 ml (1 pint) boiling water for 5 minutes, then drained, rinsed under hot running water, then drained again in a colander

1 teaspoon salt

FOR THE SAUCE
1 teaspoon Dijon mustard

½ tablespoon Tabasco (optional)

15 g (½ oz) cornflour

25 ml (1 fl oz) cold water

9 Add the prawns to the sauce and allow them to heat through and then pour into a bowl to serve.

TO SERVE

10 Spoon the rice onto a large platter and make a space in the middle. Place the bowl of prawns and sauce in the space and serve!

TIPS

- Peeled prawns can also be used for this dish.

- Do not be tempted to overcook the prawns, they only need the time advised.

- Do not hesitate to add more water to the cooking stock if it has thickened rapidly.

- The rice will cook and tenderise only if the consistency of the stock added to it is not too thick, so stick to the amounts given and only add more water if stock is too thick.

Kreides pané

Prawns pané

This is a dish that is excellent for parties of all kinds, especially children's as it helps introduce them to fresh prawns by disguising them with a fish finger-like appearance! It needs some planning but once prepared to the breadcrumb stage they can be put aside and fried when needed – waiting does not affect the result: if anything, it enhances it.

SERVES: 4

PREPARATION TIME: 30 minutes

COOKING TIME: 15 minutes

FOR THE PRAWNS
1 kg (2.2 lb) large fresh king prawns

1 teaspoon salt

½ teaspoon white pepper

FOR THE PANÉ
2 eggs, beaten

1½ tablespoons water

75 g (3 oz) plain flour

150 g (5 oz) breadcrumbs

TO PREPARE THE PRAWNS

1 Peel the prawns and leave the tail intact. Then, using a small sharp knife remove the black vein by piercing the back of each prawn and pulling it out gently.

2 Wash the prawns thoroughly under cold running water and put them in a colander to drain.

3 Using a sharp knife deepen the slit where the black vein was removed and flatten the prawn using the palm of the hand, creating a fan shape.

4 Season the prawns with salt and white pepper and arrange on a flat dish.

TO PREPARE THE PANÉ

5 Mix the beaten eggs with the water, pour into a dish and set aside.

6 Place the flour on a plate and do the same with the breadcrumbs.

7 Start by dipping the prawns first in the flour, followed by the egg mixture and lastly into the breadcrumbs, making sure that the prawns are well coated. Keep to one side until ready to cook.

TO MAKE THE TARTARE SAUCE

8 Mix the onion, parsley, pepper, gherkin (if using), salt, pepper, lemon juice and mayonnaise together, taste and adjust accordingly. Set aside.

TO COOK THE PRAWNS

9 Heat the vegetable oil in the pan and fry the prawns until they are golden brown in colour. Then drain on kitchen paper.

TO SERVE

10 Serve the prawns on a bed of shredded lettuce with lemon wedges all round decorated with parsley sprigs and with the sauce on the side.

TIPS

- The prawns can be prepared well in advance up to the breadcrumb stage and kept in the refrigerator to be fried when required.
- This dish is very versatile as a starter or for buffets and parties.
- Tabasco sauce may be added to the sauce if a more spicy flavour is required.
- *Red chilli sauce* (see p. 38) can be served as an extra dip on the side.

FOR THE TARTARE SAUCE
1 small onion, peeled and finely chopped

50 g (2 oz) chopped fresh parsley

½ red pepper, deseeded and finely chopped

1 gherkin, finely chopped (optional)

½ teaspoon salt

freshly ground black pepper to taste

50 ml (2 fl oz) lemon juice

200 g (7 oz) mayonnaise

FOR FRYING
150 ml (5 fl oz) vegetable oil

TO GARNISH
shredded lettuce

lemon wedges

sprigs of fresh parsley

Kreides bi kouzbara wa toum

Prawns in tomato and coriander sauce

SERVES: **4**

PREPARATION TIME: **30 minutes**

COOKING TIME: **20 minutes**

20 large fresh king prawns

75 ml (3 fl oz) olive oil or
vegetable ghee

1 teaspoon salt

1 teaspoon sugar

1 teaspoon white pepper

8 tomatoes, skinned and
finely chopped

225 g (8 oz) tin chopped tomatoes,
sieved

75 ml (3 fl oz) water

25 ml (1 fl oz) lemon juice

3 tablespoons *Coriander and garlic
paste* (see p. 36)

1 tablespoon Tabasco (optional)

1 teaspoon Dijon mustard

1 tablespoon chopped fresh parsley

TO GARNISH

1 teaspoon pine nuts

TO ACCOMPANY

a green salad

White rice (see p. 32)

An instant success, this recipe converts the simplest ingredients into a real treat. A word of caution, though: the prawns have to be extra large; small prawns can be used but they won't be as effective.

1 Peel the prawns and leave the tail intact. Then, using a small sharp knife remove the black vein by piercing the back of each prawn and pulling it out gently.

2 Wash the prawns thoroughly under cold running water and put them in a colander to drain.

3 Using a sharp knife deepen the slit where the black vein was removed and flatten the prawn using the palm of the hand, creating a fan shape.

4 In a heavy-based frying pan, heat the olive oil. Add the prawns to the frying pan and fry thoroughly on a high heat for a few minutes, shaking the pan instead of stirring.

5 Lower the heat to moderate, add the salt, sugar, pepper, chopped fresh tomatoes, sieved tomatoes, water and lemon juice and allow to cook together for 10 minutes, stirring occasionally.

6 Add the *Coriander and garlic paste*, mix thoroughly and allow to simmer for 5 more minutes, stirring occasionally.

7 Finally, add the Tabasco and mustard and cook for another minute. Sprinkle on the parsley, then taste and adjust the seasoning accordingly. Turn off the heat.

8 Serve immediately on a flat dish, and sprinkle with pine nuts.

TIP

• Frozen prawns can be used. Defrost them preferably overnight in the refrigerator, then wash and follow the recipe as above.

Fish in tahini sauce

This is a very simple yet tasty dish and very quick to make. I regard it as my emergency stand-by. Served with a simple salad in the summer or with potatoes in the winter, this dish proves to be not only versatile but a dish for all seasons.

SERVES: 4–5

PREPARATION TIME: 20 minutes

COOKING TIME: 20 minutes

1 kg (2.2 lb) fish fillets (cod, halibut or whatever fillets are in season) cut into 4–5 portions, then washed and dried with absorbent kitchen paper

1 teaspoon salt

½ teaspoon white pepper

½ teaspoon ground cumin

110 g (4 oz) flour

FOR FRYING

150 ml (5 fl oz) olive oil

FOR THE TAHINI SAUCE

½ teaspoon salt

275 ml (10 fl oz) tahini

110 ml (4 fl oz) cold water

150 ml (5 fl oz) lemon juice

50 g (2 oz) unsalted butter

1 large onion, peeled and finely sliced

50 g (2 oz) pine nuts (optional)

TEMPERATURE

preheat the oven to gas mark 2, 300°F (150°C)

YOU WILL ALSO NEED

an ovenproof dish

1 Mix together the salt, pepper and cumin; then use this mixture to season the fillets.

2 Put the flour into a dish and dip the fillets into it to coat them on both sides.

3 Heat the olive oil in the frying pan, and once hot add the fillets. Be careful not to overcrowd the pan. Brown on both sides, then drain on kitchen paper.

4 To make the tahini sauce, add the salt to the tahini followed by half the water. Blend well and then add the lemon juice. As it thickens, quickly add the rest of the water, mix well together and set aside.

5 In a saucepan heat the butter and then sauté the sliced onion until slightly brown. Add the tahini sauce, mix in and allow to simmer gently for a few seconds to heat through.

6 Arrange the fillets in an ovenproof dish in a layer or two, pour the sauce on top of the fillets, sprinkle over the pine nuts (if using) and place in the preheated oven for 10–12 minutes.

7 Serve with a salad or a selection of salad *mezzes* and savour the flavour.

TIPS

• Do not be tempted to overcook the fillets as they need to be moist yet tender.

• If the tahini sauce is too thick a little water may be added.

• Always taste and adjust accordingly.

• For advance preparation the fillets can be prepared up to the flouring stage (stage 2), the tahini sauce prepared and then the dish assembled later when needed.

• One tablespoon of chopped fresh coriander or parsley may be added to the sliced onion before adding the tahini sauce.

Fish fatayer

This is a great dish for when you have leftovers of cooked fish, or when you want to create a very comforting fish dish out of a bland piece of fish. It is easy yet very impressive when served with Aubergine mousakaa (pp. 87–8) or Green beans (p. 88) and a green salad – a great feast.

1 Heat a frying pan and add the butter followed by the fillets, turning them over gently. Add the salt and pepper and allow to sauté on a moderate heat for about 4–5 minutes shaking the pan gently regularly. Cool and set aside.

2 For the filling, heat the olive oil in a pan and add the sliced leek. Sauté gently to soften, add the ground coriander (if using) and the spinach, turning them over once twice without allowing them to wilt. Add the *Coriander pesto*, mix well and set aside to cool.

3 Roll out the pastry after it has come to room temperature into a large square 0.5 cm (¼ inch) thick.

4 Cut four squares out of the large square.

5 Divide the fish between the four squares, placing them neatly in the centre and topped by the rest of the filling, leaving any liquid in the pan.

6 Brush the edges of every square with beaten egg and draw the four corners neatly to the centre to form a parcel.

7 Brush the parcels all over with beaten egg and place on the lined oven tray.

8 Bake for 10 minutes or until golden brown.

9 Serve garnished with parsley sprigs and lemon wedges.

TIPS
- If frozen puff pastry is used defrost according to instructions before use.
- It is important to prepare the fish and filling, and then cool both before filling the pastry.
- Make sure any liquid is drained off before filling the parcels otherwise the pastry will not be as crispy.
- The fillings can be prepared well in advance and cooled or refrigerated to be assembled with the pastry later.

Fatayer bi samak

SERVES: **4**
PREPARATION TIME: **20 minutes**
COOKING TIME: **25 minutes**

FOR THE FISH
50 g (2 oz) unsalted butter

275 g (10 oz) cod fillets, skinned

1 teaspoon salt

½ teaspoon white pepper

FOR THE FILLING
1 tablespoon olive oil

½ leek, finely sliced

½ teaspoon ground coriander (optional)

110 g (4 oz) baby spinach

1 tablespoon *Coriander pesto* (see pp. 47–8)

FOR THE PASTRY
350 g (12 oz) puff pastry, fresh or frozen

1 egg, beaten

TO GARNISH
lemon wedges

parsley sprigs

TEMPERATURE
preheat the oven to gas mark 8, 425°F (220°C)

YOU WILL ALSO NEED
an oven tray lined with baking parchment

a small pastry brush

RICE

People are all too ready to believe the common myth that rice is difficult to cook. But I'm here to tell you it's not. What's more, rice isn't dull either. Just sample the recipes in this chapter, and you'll have your own proof. Additionally, cast your mind back to other recipes in this book that use rice as a stuffing, an accompaniment or a dessert. It really is a very versatile food indeed – made all the more interesting by those special Lebanese touches.

Vegetable rice

SERVES: 4–5

PREPARATION TIME: 30 minutes

COOKING TIME: 20 minutes

75 ml (3 fl oz) extra virgin olive oil or vegetable ghee

1 large onion, peeled and finely chopped

1 teaspoon granulated sugar

1 carrot, peeled and thinly sliced

1 tablespoon salt

1 teaspoon white pepper

1 teaspoon ground cardamom

½ teaspoon ground allspice

½ teaspoon cinnamon

1 teaspoon ground coriander

1 teaspoon saffron

½ teaspoon freshly grated nutmeg

½ teaspoon cumin

2 tomatoes, skinned and finely chopped

75 g (3 oz) tinned chickpeas, drained (optional)

½ bunch coriander, finely chopped

570 ml (1 pint) boiling water

450 g (1 lb) basmati rice, soaked in 570 ml (1 pint) boiling water for 5 minutes, then drained, rinsed under hot running water, then drained again in a colander

75 g (3 oz) frozen peas (petits pois)

TO GLAZE

2 tablespoons extra virgin olive oil

2 cloves garlic, peeled and chopped

This rice, accompanied by a salad or yoghurt dip, can be a meal in itself. It is simple yet full of flavour and with many contrasts between the different vegetables and spices. The choice of vegetables is important for this dish, which proves that rice is not boring!

1   In a large pan, heat the olive oil or ghee. Add the chopped onion and sugar and sauté until light brown. Add the carrot. Stir well.

2   Add the salt, pepper, cardamom, allspice, cinnamon, ground coriander, saffron, nutmeg and cumin and mix well.

3   Add the chopped tomatoes and stir, followed by the chickpeas, fresh coriander and some of the water. Lower the heat to medium, and allow to cook together for a few minutes.

4   Add the remaining water and once it starts boiling, add the drained rice and mix in. Then add the peas and cover with a lid. Allow to cook for a few minutes to absorb some of the liquid. Then transfer to the heated oven for 5–10 minutes.

5   Meanwhile, in a small frying pan heat 2 tablespoons of olive oil. Add the chopped garlic and sauté for a couple of minutes to flavour the oil. Do not overcook the garlic.

6   Take the rice out of the oven and pour the oil and garlic over the top. Put the lid back on without stirring the rice.

7   After 5 minutes, take off the lid and mix the rice with the handle of a wooden spoon, gently and without applying too much pressure.

8   Serve the vegetable rice on a flat dish sprinkled with the pine nuts. It can be accompanied by *Loubieh bizeit* (see p. 88) and yoghurt as a fantastic vegetarian dish. It is also ideal as an accompaniment to meat dishes and barbecues too.

TIPS

•   Do not stir the rice while it is cooking – shake the pan instead if necessary.

•   Allow the rice to stand before serving.

•   More vegetables can be added or substituted, for example spinach when in season, red or green peppers or whatever is available, but make sure the vegetables are in proportion to the rice.

- The peas do not need to be defrosted, and as long as they are added to the rice when instructed, they will cook while retaining their colour and flavour.

TO GARNISH
50 g (2 oz) pine nuts

TEMPERATURE
preheat the oven to gas mark 3,
325°F (170°C)

Vermicelli rice

Ruz bi shie'riyeh

SERVES: **4**
PREPARATION TIME: **10 minutes**
COOKING TIME: **15 minutes**

Vermicelli rice is mostly served with less strongly flavoured dishes, such as tomato-based stews and casseroles. It has a nutty taste and has a more full-bodied flavour than white rice. The real trick lies in the browning of the vermicelli. But don't worry, this recipe is foolproof – follow it and it will soon become a favourite.

2 tablespoons vegetable ghee or clarified butter

75 g (3 oz) vermicelli, broken into small pieces

350 g (12 oz) basmati rice, soaked in 570 ml (1 pint) boiling water for 5 minutes, then drained, rinsed under hot running water, then drained again in a colander

900 ml (1½ pints) boiling water

1 teaspoon salt

1   Heat the ghee or butter in a pan. Add the vermicelli and stir continuously until it is light caramel brown all over.

2   Add the drained rice to the vermicelli, and wait for a few seconds. Then stir to mix the ingredients, to coat the grains of rice with ghee and to bring everything to the same temperature.

3   Pour the boiling water on to the rice and vermicelli, and add the salt. Stir once only. Allow it to simmer until most of the water is absorbed.

TEMPERATURE
preheat the oven to gas mark 5,
375°F (190°C)

4   Put the lid on and transfer to the heated oven for 5–7 minutes. Once little holes appear in the rice, this means that it is ready.

5   Remove from the oven and allow to stand for 5 minutes before serving.

TIPS
- Butter should not be used instead of ghee, unless it is clarified butter, otherwise it will burn while browning the vermicelli and discolour the rice.
- The water must be boiling when it is added to the rice to avoid it becoming sticky.
- To achieve separated rice (*ruz mufalfal* in Arabic), getting the vermicelli and rice to the correct temperature before adding the water is essential so the water is quickly absorbed.

Aubergine and lamb makloubeh

Makloubeh means a dish that one turns upside down. It's the perfect family gathering dish. Because it's best served as soon as it is cooked and doesn't take kindly to reheating, this dish would normally be prepared on a day when all the family can sit down together at the dinner table. You can choose either aubergines or cauliflower, which are the traditional vegetables to go with the dish. If you opt for aubergine, then lamb is the recommended meat; if cauliflower is used, chicken becomes the accompaniment. Try both. They are each distinctive, and each has its own type and combination of flavours.

SERVES: 4–6

PREPARATION TIME: **40 minutes**

COOKING TIME: **1–1¼ hours**

25 ml (1 fl oz) extra virgin olive oil

1 shoulder of lamb, cut with the bone into medium-size pieces (ask your butcher to do it)

½ onion, peeled

4 whole black peppercorns

4 whole cardamom pods

2½ teaspoons salt

2.3 litres (4 pints) boiling water

2 aubergines peeled, thickly sliced and soaked in 1.75 litres (3 pints) cold, salty water for at least 1 hour

1 potato, peeled, thickly sliced and added to the aubergines in the salty water

50 g (2 oz) vegetable ghee or clarified butter

6 cloves garlic, peeled

4 tomatoes, halved

½ teaspoon white pepper

½ teaspoon cinnamon

½ teaspoon ground allspice

½ teaspoon freshly grated nutmeg

1 teaspoon ground cardamom

1 teaspoon saffron (optional)

1 tablespoon pomegranate syrup (see p. 26)

350 g (12 oz) basmati rice soaked in 570 ml (1 pint) boiling water for 5 minutes, then drained, rinsed under hot running water, then drained again in a colander

1 In a heated pan, add the olive oil followed by the lamb pieces. Sauté the meat until it is brown. Stir for 5 minutes.

2 Add the onion, whole peppercorns, cardamom pods, 1 teaspoon of salt and boiling water. Bring to the boil, cover with a lid and reduce the heat to moderate. Simmer for 40–50 minutes, checking regularly to make sure there is enough liquid in the pot until the meat is cooked through. Strain the lamb pieces from the pan and reserve the stock.

3 Meanwhile, drain and dry the aubergine and potato slices. Deep fry in oil at a temperature of 375°F (190°C) until light brown in colour. Alternatively fry in batches in your frying pan. Drain on a double layer of absorbent kitchen paper.

4 In a small frying pan, warm the ghee or butter. Add the cloves of garlic, brown slightly and remove with a slotted spoon. Add the halved tomatoes to the heated ghee. Brown them and set to one side.

5 In your round, low-handled pan, layer the lamb pieces on the base followed by the fried aubergine pieces, followed by potato slices, tomato halves and cloves of garlic, leaving a round gap in the middle.

6 Add the remaining salt, white pepper, cinnamon, allspice, nutmeg, ground cardamom and saffron (if using), followed by the pomegranate syrup and lamb stock. Put the pan on a medium heat and simmer. Bring the ingredients gently to the boil, then fill the gap in the middle of the pan with the rice. Make sure the rest of the rice completely covers the layer of vegetables. Cook for 10 minutes uncovered, then take off the heat.

YOU WILL ALSO NEED
a rounded pan (suitable for the hob
and the oven) with handles lower than
the rim of the pan to enable the
finished dish to be turned upside down

a serving plate to match the pan
in size

a deep-fat fryer or frying pan

TO ACCOMPANY
Cucumber and yoghurt salad (see
pp. 34–5) or *Olive salad* (see p. 72)

Makloubet zaher

SERVES: 4

PREPARATION TIME: 40 minutes

COOKING TIME: 1–1¼ hours

50 ml (2 fl oz) extra virgin olive oil

1 large chicken, cleaned, dried and
jointed into 8 pieces

½ onion, peeled

4 whole black peppercorns

4 whole cardamom pods

2½ teaspoons salt

2.3 litres (4 pints) boiling water

7 Cover the pan with a lid or aluminium foil and put in a heated oven for a further 12–15 minutes until all the stock has been absorbed and the rice is cooked.

8 Allow the cooked dish to stand for 20 minutes.

9 Place a large serving plate over the top of your pan and turn the whole lot over. The contents of the pan should come out in one piece on your serving dish. Sprinkle over the pine nuts and serve with the suggested salads. *Sahtane*!

TIPS

- The special pan with low handles makes it much easier to turn the dish upside down.

- If the skins of the tomatoes start to come off while they are being sautéed, peel them off as this will improve the presentation.

Cauliflower and chicken makloubeh

1 In a heated pan, add the olive oil followed by the chicken pieces. Sauté the meat until it is brown. Stir for 5 minutes.

2 Add the onion, peppercorns, cardamom pods, 1 teaspoon salt and 2.3 litres (4 pints) of boiling water. Bring to the boil, lower the heat, then cover with aluminium foil or a lid and simmer for 40–50 minutes, checking regularly to make sure there is enough liquid in the pot.

3 Once cooked, remove the chicken pieces from the pan and reserve the stock.

4 Meanwhile, drain and dry the cauliflower pieces. Deep fry in oil at a temperature of 375°F (190°C) until light brown. Alternatively fry in batches in your frying pan. Drain on a double layer of absorbent kitchen paper.

5 In a small frying pan, warm the ghee or clarified butter. Add the garlic, brown slightly and remove with a slotted spoon.

6 Layer the chicken pieces on the base of the round low-handled pan, followed by the fried cauliflower, all the way round leaving a gap in middle. Add the sautéed garlic and ghee. Add the rest of the salt, pepper, saffron (if using), ground cardamom, allspice, nutmeg, cinnamon and cumin. Add the reserved stock, place the pan on a medium heat and bring gently to the boil.

7 Place the rice in the empty gap, then cover the cauliflower completely with the rest. Make sure there is enough stock to cover the rice. Allow to simmer gently for 10 minutes uncovered, until some of the stock is absorbed.

8 Cover the pan with a lid or aluminium foil and cook in the oven for a further 12–15 minutes.

9 Take out of the oven and allow to stand for 20 minutes.

10 Turn out as described for the aubergine version. Scatter with the pine nuts and serve with the suggested salads.

TIPS

- Soaking the cauliflower in salted water reduces the amount of oil absorbed during frying and reduces the occasional bloated feeling one suffers after eating cauliflower!

- Covering the pot while the chicken is being cooked is vital as it cooks the chicken without the stock evaporating too much.

- Vermicelli pasta can be added to the rice: break the vermicelli into small pieces, brown in 50 ml (2 fl oz) oil or ghee and mix with the rice.

- Do not add the rice to the pan before the stock starts to boil, as the temperature of the stock has to be high so that the rice absorbs it quickly.

1 large cauliflower, cut into florets and soaked in 1.1 litres (2 pints) of cold salty water for at least 1 hour

2 tablespoons vegetable ghee or clarified butter

6 cloves garlic, peeled

½ teaspoon white pepper

1 teaspoon saffron (optional)

1 teaspoon ground cardamom

½ teaspoon ground allspice

½ teaspoon freshly grated nutmeg

½ teaspoon cinnamon

1 teaspoon cumin

350 g (12 oz) basmati rice, soaked in 1.1 litres (2 pints) boiling water for 5 minutes, then drained, rinsed under hot running water, then drained again in a colander

TO GARNISH
75 g (3 oz) pine nuts, sautéed

TEMPERATURE
preheat the oven to gas mark 4, 350°F (180°C)

YOU WILL ALSO NEED
a rounded pan (suitable for the hob and the oven) with handles lower than the rim of the pan to enable the finished dish to be turned upside down

a serving plate to match the pan in size

a deep-fat fryer or frying pan

TO ACCOMPANY
Cucumber and yoghurt salad (see pp. 34–5), or *Lebanese caesar salad* (see pp. 72–3)

Rice and lamb in a pot

SERVES: **4**

PREPARATION TIME: **10 minutes**

COOKING TIME: **30 minutes**

50 ml (2 fl oz) extra virgin olive oil

12 cutlets of lamb, cleaned and with fat removed

1 teaspoon granulated sugar

1½ teaspoons salt

1 teaspoon white pepper

1 teaspoon ground cardamom

1 teaspoon saffron

½ teaspoon allspice

½ teaspoon cinnamon

1.1 litres (2 pints) boiling water

2 tablespoons butter ghee or vegetable ghee

5 cloves garlic, peeled and finely sliced

450 g (1 lb) basmati rice, soaked in 570 ml (1 pint) boiling water for 5 minutes, then drained, rinsed under hot running water, then drained again in a colander

TO GARNISH
50 g (2 oz) pine nuts

TEMPERATURE
preheat the oven to gas mark 4, 350°F (180°C)

YOU WILL ALSO NEED
a heavy pot with a heavy lid, suitable for hob and oven

TO ACCOMPANY
Tabbouleh (see pp. 70–1), *Loubieh bizeit* (see p. 88)

In Arabic Kidrah *is derived from the noun* kider *which means 'pot'. The feminine form of this noun is* kidreh, *and nomads used the name for this dish cooked in a pot. You will need a heavy pot or pan with a heavy lid, so that the rice can be cooked to the required texture and flavour in the minimum amount of time. To me this is the perfect example of a successful meal where little effort is needed. The pot does the work for me, and the meat is easy and quick to cook.*

1 In your heavy pot, heat the olive oil. When hot add the lamb cutlets and brown on all sides on a high heat. This will take about 5–10 minutes, and it is best if you fry them in two batches.

2 Once all the cutlets are browned, put them back into the pan and add the sugar, salt, pepper, cardamom, saffron, allspice and cinnamon. Stir to coat the meat pieces with the spices.

3 Add the boiling water, reduce the heat to moderate and cover the pan with its heavy lid.

4 Heat the ghee in a small frying pan and when hot add the garlic slices. Sauté to cook lightly without burning, then add everything to the cooking cutlets and stock.

5 Leave the meat to simmer for 15 more minutes, then add the rice and stir. Put the lid back on for 3 minutes so that the rice absorbs some of the liquid.

6 Transfer the pan to the heated oven and leave for 10 minutes.

7 Take out of the oven, pile everything onto a flat dish and put the gorgeous, succulent cutlets on top. Scatter over the pine nuts. The house will be filled with the wonderful aromas of nomadic cooking!

TIPS

• A shoulder of lamb, cut up with the bones (ask your butcher to do it, into about 8 pieces) or even a leg of lamb, can be used instead but double the cooking time to ensure that the meat is cooked before the rice is added.

• Ghee is essential for the taste of this dish – which is not for the weight conscious!

• The pot or pan is the most important item in this recipe. Unless you have the right sort of pan, you won't get the taste and result required.

• Prepare this dish with immediate serving in mind as reheating does not suit it.

Lentils and rice

This is the vegetarian alternative to meat and rice. It is wholesome and delicious, especially when served hot out of the oven.

1   In a large pan, cover the lentils with 1.75 litres (3 pints) of hot water. Bring to the boil then reduce the heat to moderate, and allow the lentils to simmer.

2   In a frying pan, heat the olive oil. Add the onions, followed by the sugar and allow to caramelise gently.

3   Pour the caramelised onions into the cooking lentils. Cover the pot and continue to simmer for about 30 minutes, stirring occasionally.

4   Once the lentils are soft and tender, add the salt, pepper, cinnamon, saffron (if using), cumin, allspice and nutmeg and mix well with the lentils.

5   Add the rice to the lentils along with a little more hot water if necessary, and mix in. Cover the pot and cook until most of the liquid is absorbed.

6   Meanwhile, make the glaze. Heat the olive oil in a small frying pan, add the garlic slices and sauté on a moderate heat. Add to the rice and lentils straight away.

7   Transfer the pan to the oven to cook the rice thoroughly for a further 5–7 minutes.

8   Serve the lentils and rice on a flat plate, garnished with the caramelised onion slices and accompanied by one of the suggested salads.

TIPS

- Tinned lentils can be used instead of fresh. If using, add them just before the rice is added to the stock.

- Fried onions are the traditional garnish to this dish. Make sure you slice them very thinly.

- Do not be tempted to mix the sautéed garlic into the rice and lentils. Just leave them on the top, put the lid of the pan back on and transfer to the oven straight away.

Mudardarah

SERVES: **4–6**
PREPARATION TIME: **20 minutes**
COOKING TIME: **50 minutes**

150 g (5 oz) green lentils, washed thoroughly

1.75 litres (3 pints) hot water

75 ml (3 fl oz) extra virgin olive oil

2 onions, peeled and sliced

1 teaspoon granulated sugar

1½ teaspoons salt

½ teaspoon white pepper

½ teaspoon cinnamon

1 teaspoon saffron (optional)

½ teaspoon cumin

½ teaspoon ground allspice

½ teaspoon freshly grated nutmeg

450 g (1 lb) basmati rice soaked in 570 ml (1 pint) boiling water for 5 minutes, then drained, rinsed under hot running water, then drained again in a colander

FOR THE GLAZE
3 cloves garlic, peeled and finely sliced

25 ml (1 fl oz) extra virgin olive oil

TO GARNISH
1 onion, peeled and thinly sliced, then shallow-fried until brown and caramelised, then drained on absorbent kitchen paper

TEMPERATURE
preheat the oven to gas mark 4, 350°F (180°C)

TO ACCOMPANY
Cucumber and yoghurt salad (see pp. 34–5) or *Olive salad* (see p. 72)

Lamb with rice and yoghurt sauce

SERVES: **4–5**

PREPARATION TIME: **40 minutes**

COOKING TIME: **1–1½ hours**

FOR THE MEAT

900 g (2 lb) shoulder of lamb cut with the bones into 8 pieces (ask your butcher to do this), washed and dried

4 whole cardamom pods

4 whole black peppercorns

1 small onion, peeled

1 teaspoon salt

2.3 litres (4 pints) boiling water

FOR THE SAUCE

900 g (2 lb) yoghurt, preferably *Home-made* (see p. 34), or Greek yoghurt

1 teaspoon salt

½ teaspoon white pepper

⅔ meat stock from the cooked lamb

25 g (1 oz) cornflour mixed with 50 ml (2 fl oz) cold water to form a paste

2 tablespoons ghee or clarified butter

4 cloves garlic, peeled and crushed

FOR THE BASE

⅓ meat stock from the cooked lamb

275 ml (10 fl oz) of the yoghurt sauce

¼ teaspoon salt

¼ teaspoon white pepper

3 pitta breads or *Halabis* (see pp. 211–13), opened up and cut into small 2.5 cm squares, then toasted under a grill until crisp and light brown

Mansaf is a Bedouin rather than Lebanese dish, but as I cook it at my restaurant for special and important clients, I decided to include it in this book. It is a celebratory dish that encourages communal eating. It is very social yet basic as it is normally eaten using the hands because one is supposed to grab the three layers on the tray, including the meat, and eat it all in one mouthful. This is very practical, but rather traditional! Mansaf has different versions but the principle of the recipe is the same. The traditional recipe uses kishk, a dried form of yoghurt which is spiced, creamed and then dried into a ball. It is widely available in the Middle East, and here in liquid form in jars – although this is not as effective. I have therefore devised this method which is just as tasty as if you are using the genuine Middle Eastern kishk. It is easy to follow and you won't need to send out a search party for the ingredients! I hope that you will find it as satisfying and comforting as it is supposed to be.

TO PREPARE THE MEAT

1 Place the meat pieces in a deep pan with the cardamom pods, peppercorns, onion and salt. Add the boiling water.

2 Bring back to the boil, then cover with a lid and lower the heat to moderate. Allow to simmer for 40–50 minutes.

3 Once the meat has tenderised, remove it from the stock, place in a dish and cover. Set to one side, reserving the stock.

4 Divide the meat stock into two jugs or bowls, two thirds in one and one third in the other.

TO PREPARE THE YOGHURT SAUCE

5 In a pan, put the yoghurt, salt and pepper, and heat gently, stirring constantly.

6 Add two thirds of your reserved stock to the yoghurt and cook gently together.

7 As the liquid reaches boiling point, add the cornflour paste to thicken the sauce slightly. Do this slowly as you may not need to add it all, depending on the type of yoghurt used.

8 Heat the ghee or clarified butter in a frying pan. Fry the garlic to cook, but not to brown, then add half to the yoghurt sauce (reserve the other half for use later). Stir and allow to simmer for a few minutes, then add the meat pieces and allow to cook together. After a few minutes, turn off the heat.

TO PREPARE THE BASE

9 Take the second batch of reserved stock, pour into a pan and simmer on a moderate heat. Into it, add 275 ml (10 fl oz) of the prepared yoghurt sauce. Add the salt and white pepper and the reserved sautéed garlic and ghee mixture, and simmer gently for 15 minutes. Take off the heat and set aside.

TO PREPARE THE RICE

10 In a pan, heat the ghee or clarified butter. Add the rice, and coat gently with the ghee on a high heat. Add the salt and boiling water, stir and cover with aluminium foil or a lid. Leave to simmer on moderate heat until almost all the water is absorbed.

11 Transfer the pan to the oven for 5 minutes (the rice is ready when little holes start to appear in it). Take out and set aside.

12 Place the toasted pittas or *Halabi*s in an ovenproof dish, pour over the base sauce to soak them and leave in the oven for a few minutes.

FOR THE GARNISH

13 Heat the ghee or olive oil in a small frying pan and add the almonds and then the pine nuts. Fry until light brown. (The pine nuts won't take as long as the almonds.)

TO ASSEMBLE THE MANSAF

14 Take your warm, soaked pittas out of the oven, cover them with rice and place the cooked meat pieces on top of the rice. Drizzle the whole mountainous effect with the yoghurt sauce, and scatter on the nuts.

FOR THE RICE

2 tablespoons ghee or clarified butter

450 g (1 lb) basmati rice soaked in 570 ml (1 pint) boiling water for 5 minutes, then drained, rinsed under hot running water, then drained again in a colander

1 teaspoon salt

900 ml (1½ pints) boiling water

TO GARNISH

2 tablespoons vegetable ghee or olive oil

50 g (2 oz) blanched almonds

50 g (2 oz) pine nuts

TEMPERATURE

preheat the oven to gas mark 4, 350°F (180°C)

TO SERVE

15 Serve immediately with yoghurt sauce on the side.

16 All you need to accompany this feast is a few green olives and some sliced tomatoes.

TIPS

• The pitta bread has to be toasted before it is soaked in the base sauce so that it retains its shape. It also gives a lighter texture to the dish.

• The base sauce will need to be reheated before it is poured over the toasted bread.

• If the yoghurt sauce is too thick at any stage of cooking, do not hesitate to add some water. The sauce should be smooth but not too thick.

GRILLS

Grilled foods are easy and quick. They also lend themselves to a range of accompaniments. They require little preparation, and can be cooked in minutes. You can use either the grill on your oven, an outdoor barbecue or a griddle if you have one. I think a combination of using the griddle first and then the oven grill works best. An outdoor barbecue, weather permitting, will allow you to grill a larger quantity of meat at the same time. The choice is yours, and whatever you decide you can be assured of a tasty result, as long as the meat, chicken or fish used is fresh and of great quality. A marinade will complement the item being grilled and enhances its flavour as long as the proportions are right. Using too much marinade can cause problems, as unless it is shaken off the meat before cooking, it can burn the outside before the inside is cooked. Take all these points into account when marinating or grilling anything and always remember that practice makes perfect and that you must start somewhere!

Grilled chicken

Shish taouk *captures the true taste of grilled Lebanese chicken at its best. The Garlic sauce is the marinade and the main ingredient for this recipe's success.*

1 In a bowl mix the chicken breast fillets with the *Garlic sauce*, paprika, salt, pepper, lemon juice and olive oil. Chill for at least 1 hour or preferably overnight in the refrigerator.

2 Thread the meat on to the skewers and put the skewers onto the hot griddle pan. Grill each skewer for 1 minute on each side.

3 Place the skewers on the oven tray, brush with any left over marinade and grill for a further 6 minutes, turning halfway.

4 Serve the chicken with the suggested accompaniments. Enjoy!

TIPS

- Alternatively, all the cooking can be completed under the grill – just add another minute to the cooking time in step 3.

- The grill should be hot but not so hot that it burns the chicken.

SERVES: 4

PREPARATION TIME: **15 minutes, plus at least 1 hour for marinating**

COOKING TIME: **15 minutes**

FOR THE CHICKEN
700 g (1½ lb) chicken breast fillets, diced into 2 cm (¾ inch) pieces

50 g (1 oz) *Garlic sauce* (see p. 37)

½ teaspoon paprika

1 teaspoon salt

½ teaspoon white pepper

½ teaspoon freshly ground black pepper

75 ml (3 fl oz) lemon juice

50 ml (2 fl oz) extra virgin olive oil

TEMPERATURE
preheat the grill to its medium setting

YOU WILL ALSO NEED
a griddle pan preheated for 5 minutes if you have one

16 skewers for grilling

an oven tray lined with aluminium foil

TO ACCOMPANY
Fattoush (see p. 69), *Aubergine dip* (see pp. 74–5), mixed pickles (see pp. 40–4) and pitta breads (see p. 211)

Chicken wings

This is a great grill item. Chicken wings are a good starter or accompaniment to different mezzes, or just eat them on their own for a snack or light meal. Marinating chicken wings enhances their flavour immensely, but even if they are plain as long as they are fresh and clean they are delicious. It has become fashionable to skin chicken wings, but I personally disagree with that, as most of the flavour of the wing is in the skin. Make sure that the chicken wings are grilled well, and don't worry about the calories – some things are worth the naughtiness!

SERVES: 4 as a starter

**PREPARATION TIME: 10 minutes,
plus 1 hour for marinating**

COOKING TIME: 7 minutes

16 chicken wings

1 teaspoon salt

½ teaspoon white pepper

½ teaspoon paprika

25 ml (1 fl oz) lemon juice

25 ml (1 fl oz) extra virgin olive oil

½ teaspoon freshly ground
black pepper

TEMPERATURE
preheat the grill to the highest setting

YOU WILL ALSO NEED
a griddle pan preheated for 5 minutes
if you have one

4 skewers

1 Clean and wash the chicken wings, then dry them with absorbent kitchen paper.

2 Mix together the salt, white pepper, paprika, lemon juice, olive oil and freshly ground black pepper. Coat the wings in the marinade and leave for at least 1 hour.

3 Put 4 wings on each skewer and put on the heated griddle pan.

4 Grill the wings for 1 minute on each side to colour them, then place the griddle pan under the oven grill for 5 more minutes, turning the skewers over half way.

5 Serve with the rest of your chosen *mezze*, or on their own.

TIPS

• Alternatively, all the cooking can be completed under the grill – just add a couple of minutes to the cooking time in step 4.

• Freezing the wings is another convenience worth considering. Freeze fresh chicken wings rather than buying them already frozen, as the taste will be much better.

• Chicken wings behave well on reheating, so they can be cooked and kept for later.

Lamb kebabs

This is a mild, typically Lebanese version of lamb kebabs, but it also provides the base for many other dishes so it's worth being familiar with.

1 In a food processor, mix together the lamb, onion, red pepper, parsley, cinnamon, salt, white pepper and olive oil on a pulse motion without over-blending. Cover and chill for half an hour or so to make skewering easier.

2 Form the mixture into 12 balls.

3 Insert the skewer into the centre of each ball and then flatten to form a long kebab.

4 Place the skewers on the heated griddle pan. Allow to brown on one side for about 1 minute, then turn over and brown the other side.

5 Then place the griddle pan under the oven grill for 4 minutes, turning once halfway.

6 Serve with *Tabla* and *Perfect hommous*.

TIPS

• Alternatively, all the cooking can be completed under the grill – just add a couple of minutes to the cooking time in step 5.

• The skewers can be prepared and kept in the refrigerator on a tray covered with cling film until you are ready to grill them.

• Wetting the hands with cold water before putting the meat on the skewers helps stop the meat from sticking to the palm of the hand.

• Wearing cooking gloves will help keep the meat fresh and is more hygienic.

• The basic mixture will keep very well in the coldest part of the refrigerator for a few days.

• The kebab can be long or short, according to the skewers used.

• Garlic can be added to the mixture. Peel a clove and finely chop it in the food processor before anything else and then add the rest of the ingredients. You may think it enhances the meat. I prefer it without, though.

Kafta halabiyeh

SERVES: **4**

PREPARATION TIME: **20 minutes**

COOKING TIME: **15 minutes**

700 g (1½ lb) lamb, finely minced

1 medium onion, peeled and very finely chopped

1 red pepper, deseeded and very finely chopped

½ bunch flat leaf parsley, finely chopped

½ teaspoon cinnamon

1½ teaspoons salt

1 teaspoon white pepper

1 tablespoon extra virgin olive oil

TEMPERATURE
preheat the grill to the highest setting

YOU WILL ALSO NEED
a griddle pan preheated for 5 minutes if you have one

12 skewers for grilling

TO ACCOMPANY
Tabla (see p. 46) and *Perfect hommous* (see p. 66)

Kafta bisineyeh

Because the basic Kafta halabiyeh *mixture (see p. 183) can be stored in the refrigerator ahead of use, it is a fantastic standby. Here it is cooked on a tray with other ingredients on top, which add to the flavour and enhance it visually.* Kafta *can perhaps be a little boring, but with a few additions it becomes a real treat. As it is very popular with children, we shall keep it simple and not too spicy.*

SERVES: **4**

PREPARATION TIME: **20 minutes plus 1 hour for soaking the potato slices**

COOKING TIME: **40 minutes**

FOR THE BASIC KAFTA
HALABIYEH MIXTURE
follow the ingredients in the previous
recipe in step 1

FOR THE KAFTA BISINEYEH
8 beef tomatoes, sliced

½ teaspoon salt

½ teaspoon white pepper

½ teaspoon cinnamon

25 ml (1 fl oz) extra virgin olive oil

50 ml (2 fl oz) lemon juice

50 g (2 oz) unsalted butter, diced

2 potatoes, peeled, thinly sliced and
soaked in a bowl of salted water for at
least 1 hour

TEMPERATURE
preheat the oven to gas mark 7,
425°F (220°C)

YOU WILL ALSO NEED
a shallow baking tray, 15 x 25 cm
(6 x 10 inches)

a deep-fat fryer or frying pan

TO ACCOMPANY
Tahini salad (see pp. 73–4) and lots
of pitta or *Halabi* bread
(see pp. 211–13)

1 Take your prepared *Kafta halabiyeh* mixture and press it into the base of your baking tray, so that it forms a complete lining.

2 Slice the tomatoes and layer them on top of the meat mixture. Season with salt, white pepper and cinnamon, and then drizzle over the olive oil and lemon juice. Scatter the diced butter evenly all over the meat.

3 Place in the preheated oven, uncovered, for 25 minutes.

4 Meanwhile, drain and dry the potato slices on absorbent kitchen paper and fry them in the deep-fat fryer at 350°F (180°C) or in your frying pan until they are light golden brown

5 Put the potato slices on top of the cooking *kafta* and leave to cook for 5 more minutes. Take out of the oven when everything is slightly browned.

6 Serve with the *Tahini salad* and breads.

TIP

• The potatoes are a great enhancement to the *kafta*, so try not to leave them out.

Grilled lamb Lebanese-style

Translated into English, Lahem mashwi *means 'grilled meat'. As this is a Lebanese dish, the meat used must be lamb. Beef is used sometimes, but usually the best cuts of lamb are used. The quality of the meat, as well as the size of the meat cubes, are very important factors to consider. This recipe can be grilled on the barbecue in summer or whenever the weather allows, but I have made allowances for other times of year. If you are cooking inside, a griddle pan is a must, as it is used to prepare the meat before it goes under the oven grill. The result will be just as good as a barbecue, plus you can be guaranteed good weather!*

1 In a large bowl, mix the cubed lamb pieces with the salt, pepper and olive oil. Add the prepared shallots and tomatoes, turning them gently so that they stay intact but are mixed in properly.

2 Thread the seasoned meat cubes alternately with the shallot pieces on to skewers. Keep 4 skewers for the tomatoes, as these are best grilled separately.

3 Put each skewer on the griddle pan and grill for 1 minute on each side. Then place the skewers on the oven tray under the oven grill for 4 or 5 minutes.

4 Serve the skewers on a large platter, surrounded by *Tabla* and rice and with a green salad on the side.

TIPS

- Alternatively, all the cooking can be completed under the grill – just add a couple of minutes to the cooking time in step 3.

- The lamb cubes should be about 2 cm (¾ inch) square, not bigger, to ensure that the meat cooks evenly.

- You need small onions or shallots for this recipe to ensure that they cook through properly in a short time. They are also milder and sweeter and enhance the meat.

- The tomatoes can be of any size, as long as they are cut so that they don't lose their shape while they are being grilled. You can leave the small ones whole.

- Once the meat is grilled, take it out of the oven and serve as quickly as possible as otherwise it will dry out.

Lahem mashwi

SERVES: **4**
PREPARATION TIME: **20 minutes**
COOKING TIME: **15 minutes**

900 g (2 lb) leg of lamb, boned, fat removed and cubed into 2 cm (¾ inch) pieces

1 teaspoon salt

1 teaspoon white pepper

50 ml (2 fl oz) olive oil

275 g (10 oz) shallots, peeled and halved lengthways

10 tomatoes, cut into quarters

TEMPERATURE
preheat the grill to its highest setting

YOU WILL ALSO NEED
a griddle pan preheated for 5 minutes if you have one

20 skewers for grilling

an oven tray

TO ACCOMPANY
Tabla (see p. 46), *Tahini salad* (see pp. 73–4), *White rice* (see p. 32)

DESSERTS AND CAKES

Who doesn't find desserts and cakes comforting? And if people have never tried the recipes in this chapter, then I would enthusiastically encourage them to do so. There's nothing more wholesome than a rice pudding, for example. There's nothing simpler to serve with your morning coffee than a slice of cake. And there's nothing quicker to prepare for guests than vermicelli. I guarantee, even those who claim they don't have a sweet tooth won't be able to resist!

Muhallabiya

SERVES: **4–5**

PREPARATION TIME: **10 minutes**

COOKING TIME: **15 minutes**

570 ml (1 pint) full-cream milk

50 ml (2 fl oz) orange blossom water
(see p. 25)

75 g (3 oz) granulated sugar

2 tablespoons cornflour, mixed with
50 ml (2 fl oz) cold water to
form a paste

TO GARNISH
chopped pistachio nuts and
desiccated coconut

Syrup (optional – see pp. 45–6)

YOU WILL ALSO NEED
individual bowls for serving or
one flat pie dish

Lebanese milk pudding

Muhallabiya *is very simple but is the best end to a Lebanese meal. It seals the palate with sweet satisfaction and is also light, not overpowering or heavy.*

1   Put the milk in a heavy-based saucepan. Add orange blossom water and sugar. Bring gently to the boil, then whisk in the cornflour paste until the liquid thickens.

2   Remove from the heat and pour into individual dishes or a single pie dish. Put to one side until cool, then chill in the refrigerator for at least 1 hour.

3   Serve scattered with chopped pistachio nuts and desiccated coconut.

TIPS

* Skimmed milk can be used, but the result will not be as creamy.
* Fresh cream can be added to the milk to make the pudding more creamy, but I think it is creamy enough just with full-cream milk.
* Do not add the cornflour paste before the milk comes to the boil.
* The syrup can be served on the side – sweet and delicious.

Ruz bil haleeb

SERVES: **4–5**

PREPARATION TIME: **10 minutes**

COOKING TIME: **40 minutes**

75 g (3 oz) pudding (short grain) rice

150 ml (5 fl oz) boiling water

900 ml (1½ pints) full-cream milk

50 ml (2 fl oz) orange blossom water
(see p. 25)

75 g (3 oz) granulated sugar

TO GARNISH
¼ teaspoon cinnamon (optional)

YOU WILL ALSO NEED
individual glasses for serving or an
oval dish, 600–900 ml (1–1½ pints)
capacity

Rice pudding

*The most comforting puddings can be the simplest with the most basic
ingredients. Rice pudding is a prime example.*

1 Place the rice and water in a pan and cook on a moderate heat until
the water is almost all absorbed and the rice soft.

2 Add the milk and the orange blossom water, and stir. Simmer gently
for about 40 minutes stirring regularly until the rice has thickened in
the milk and become heavy.

3 Add the sugar and stir for a few minutes until it dissolves.

4 Pour into individual glasses or oval dish and set to one side to cool to
room temperature.

5 Chill in the refrigerator for at least 1 hour. Sprinkle with cinnamon (if
using) and serve.

TIPS

• Pudding rice is best for this pudding, so make sure you use it.

• The full-cream milk provides the creaminess essential for this pudding.

• Throughout cooking the heat should be low to moderate.

• Do not worry if the rice has not absorbed all the milk; it will continue to
absorb it while it is cooling and setting.

Pancakes

These are very popular during Ramadan, the fasting month, as the prime dessert, because of their high energy content and natural ingredients needed while fasting. The pancakes are sold in special shops during Ramadan, but the filling and cooking is done at home.

TO PREPARE THE PANCAKES

1 Dissolve the yeast and sugar in the lukewarm water in a jug and let it stand for 10 minutes.

2 Whisk the yeast mixture and dried milk (if using) into the flour until it is the consistency of thin batter. Add the vanilla essence, cover it and allow to prove for half an hour, covered and in a warm place.

3 Meanwhile, prepare the fillings.

4 In a bowl mix the ricotta cheese with the sugar and coconut and set aside.

5 In another bowl mix the chopped walnuts with the sugar, coconut and cinnamon and set aside.

6 Make sure the griddle or heavy non-stick pan is heated through, then put it on a low heat ready for cooking.

7 Pour the batter mixture into the milk jug and, using the soup ladle, ladle out circles of the batter onto the griddle or frying pan 4 cm in diameter. You can fit on about 4 at once. Wait until they form bubbles on the top – this should take about half a minute. Then gently scrape off the pancakes and put them onto the parchment covered tray. Repeat until you have used all the batter.

8 To stuff the pancakes, take one corner and fold it in half. Put 1 teaspoon of either filling in the centre and seal both ends of the pancake together, creating a semi-circle. Repeat, sharing the pancakes equally between the two fillings.

TO COOK THE STUFFED PANCAKES

9 Heat the ghee or corn oil in a deep frying pan. Add a few of the pancakes, turning them over quickly so that they brown lightly and are heated through. Remove and place in the bowl of cold syrup.

Kataef

MAKES: **30 pancakes**
PREPARATION TIME: **25 minutes plus proving time**
COOKING TIME: **30 minutes**

FOR THE BATTER
1 tablespoon dried yeast or 50 g (2 oz) fresh yeast

2 teaspoons caster sugar

450 ml (18 fl oz) lukewarm water

1 tablespoon dried milk (optional)

350 g (10 oz) plain flour, sifted

1 teaspoon vanilla essence

FOR THE FILLINGS
Cheese
75 g (3 oz) ricotta cheese

50 g (2 oz) caster sugar

25 g (1 oz) desiccated coconut (optional)

Walnut
75 g (3 oz) walnuts, roughly chopped

50 g (2 oz) caster sugar

25 g (1 oz) desiccated coconut

½ teaspoon cinnamon

FOR COOKING THE PANCAKES
4 tablespoons ghee or corn oil

TO SERVE
150 ml (6 fl oz) cold *Syrup* (see pp. 45–6) poured into a bowl into which the *kataef* can be dipped

TO GARNISH
chopped pistachio nuts

TO SERVE

10 Remove the pancakes from the syrup, arrange on a platter and serve with a sprinkling of chopped pistachios, and some more *Syrup* for dipping as required.

TIPS

- Fresh yeast can be used thus: replace the dried yeast with 50 g (2 oz) of fresh yeast and reduce the standing time to 10 minutes.

- Add some water to the proven batter if necessary. The mixture should not be too thick, as otherwise the pancakes will be thick and heavy.

- Both the cheese and walnut stuffing can be served, or just one kind, according to your own taste.

- *Kataef* can be filled with cream, but they should be smaller and the cream should be whipped and the *Syrup* served just on the side instead.

- When lifting the pancake off the griddle, be sure that it is cooked – otherwise the batter will stick to the griddle and make it dirty.

- The *kataef* can be baked. Arrange them on a baking tray, dot with butter or ghee and bake in an oven preheated to gas mark 5, 375°F (190°C) for 10–15 minutes, then dip in syrup and serve garnished with ground pistachios.

Oum ali

This is a breakfast, lunch or dinner treat, an absolutely heavenly combination. Once the pastry is made it can be kept in an airtight container to be used when needed. This dessert originates with Egyptian nomads. It is very popular in the Middle East. Please try my updated version.

TO PREPARE THE PASTRY

1 Cut the puff pastry into halves and roll out each half thinly.

2 Place on the baking tray and bake for 5–7 minutes until light to mid-brown.

3 Leave to cool, then flake off the top two layers of pastry. Put to one side.

YOU WILL ALSO NEED
heavy, non-stick frying pan or griddle heated for 5 minutes prior to using

3 trays, lined with parchment paper

a spatula

milk jug

small soup ladle

SERVES: **6**
PREPARATION TIME: **40 minutes**
COOKING TIME: **10 minutes**

FOR THE PASTRY
175 g (6 oz) puff pastry, fresh or frozen

FOR THE FILLING
50 g (2 oz) walnuts, shelled

50 g (2 oz) blanched almonds

25 g (1 oz) desiccated coconut

25 g (1 oz) sultanas

½ teaspoon cinnamon (optional)

570 ml (1 pint) full-cream milk

2 tablespoons granulated or
brown sugar

110 ml (4 fl oz) double cream

1 tablespoon brown sugar for
sprinkling

TEMPERATURE
preheat the oven to gas mark 7,
425°F (220°C)

YOU WILL ALSO NEED
2 oven trays

6 individual heatproof pudding dishes
(8 cm ramekin dishes)

4 Replace the remaining soft (uncooked) pastry in the oven until it too is crisp and can be flaked. Cool, flake and put to one side.

5 Repeat with the other half of the pastry until it is all flaked.

TO PREPARE THE FILLING

6 In the food processor, pulse the walnuts and set to one side. Then pulse the almonds. Mix them together in a bowl. Add the coconut and sultanas and set aside.

TO ASSEMBLE THE OUM ALI

7 Take 6 heatproof individual pudding dishes. Put 1 tablespoon of flaked pastry on the bottom, followed by 1 tablespoon of filling. Sprinkle with a little cinnamon.

8 Add another tablespoon of flaked pastry on top of the filling.

9 Bring the milk and sugar to the boil. Allow it to froth slightly, then pour over each dish until the contents are floating in the milk. Top each dish with 1 tablespoon of cream. Finally, sprinkle with the brown sugar.

10 Heat the grill to the highest setting. Place the ramekins under the grill for a minute or two until the top slightly caramelises.

11 Serve immediately.

TIPS

- Do not cut down on the creaminess of milk or omit the cream; both are essential for the required result.

- Do not be tempted to miss out the flaking the pastry stage. Otherwise the pastry won't be as light and crispy.

- When the milk is added, make sure that it is frothing and that it fills the dishes – the pastry will soak it up soon enough.

- Any leftover pastry or filling can be stored in an airtight container for later use.

SERVES: **4**

PREPARATION TIME: **10 minutes**

COOKING TIME: **10 minutes**

25 g (1 oz) clarified butter or
butter ghee

275 g (10 oz) vermicelli,
roughly broken

570 ml (1 pint) boiling water

½ teaspoon salt

1 tablespoon clarified butter or
butter ghee (optional)

110 g (4 oz) granulated sugar

TO GARNISH
1 tablespoon ground pistachio nuts

Vermicelli with sugar

*This pudding proves that simple, quality ingredients and a little bit of thought
can yield something heavenly and satisfying with a minimum effort.
Vermicelli is widely available nowadays. This recipe used to be my mother's
standby in an emergency. Whenever guests turned up unexpectedly at our
house, or there was a social afternoon at home, within five minutes or so my
mother would have prepared and be serving this instant miracle!*

1 Heat a large saucepan. Add the clarified butter or butter ghee and
when it has melted add the vermicelli.

2 Stir continuously until the vermicelli is light brown. Then add the
boiling water and salt. Lower the heat. Cover the pan and allow the
water to cook the pasta.

3 Before the water is totally absorbed, add the extra ghee or butter and
sugar. Mix together, then turn off the heat.

4 Serve on flat plates with ground pistachios as a topping.

TIPS

• Corn oil can be used for browning the vermicelli, but the taste will not be
the same.

• You should aim to make the vermicelli a caramel colour.

• Stir the vermicelli continuously while browning it to make sure it browns
evenly and does not burn.

• This dish needs to be served immediately to the waiting crowd, as it must
be smooth, glossy and sweet.

Namourah

MAKES: **20 squares**

PREPARATION TIME: **15 minutes plus
30 minutes waiting time**

COOKING TIME: **syrup: 15 minutes;
baking: 40–50 minutes**

*Namourah is one of the simplest puddings to make in Middle Eastern
cookery. It can vary in texture and lightness but the flavour will remain the
same. The recipe must be followed closely, as although the process is easy,
it is essential that the amounts of the ingredients are in proportion in order to
create the right combination of density and lightness.*

TO COOK THE SYRUP

1 In a medium-sized saucepan pour in the water followed by the sugar and mix together. Then add the lemon juice and orange blossom water.

2 Allow the syrup to simmer on a moderate to low heat for 10–12 minutes until it turns yellowish and slightly thick.

3 Take off the heat and set aside to cool.

TO PREPARE THE NAMOURAH

4 In a large bowl, mix the semolina and ghee or butter by rubbing it between your fingers until all of it is incorporated into the semolina.

5 Add the dried milk (if using), coconut and sugar and mix thoroughly.

6 Add the orange blossom water, yoghurt and bicarbonate of soda, mix together and then pour into the greased cake tin.

7 Leave to rest for half an hour, while you preheat the oven.

8 Cut the uncooked *Namourah* into squares, and put an almond in the centre of each square.

9 Put the cake tin in the oven and bake for 15–20 minutes until golden brown in colour.

10 Remove the tin from the oven, and while the *Namourah* is still hot, cut through the slices again and return to the oven for a further 10–12 minutes to brown further.

11 Take the tin out of the oven and pour the prepared syrup over the *Namourah*.

12 Allow the syrup to soak in and be absorbed before serving.

TIPS

• The desiccated coconut can be omitted, but it adds texture to the *Namourah*.

• A spring form cake tin will make it easier to remove the pieces of namourah.

• Resting the dough in the tin is vital, as it helps the semolina soak up the liquid and form the dough base.

• Put a tray under the cake tin before you pour over the syrup.

• It may look like a lot of syrup, but if you leave it for an hour or so the cake will soak it all up.

FOR THE SYRUP
175 ml (6 fl oz) water

250 g (9 oz) granulated sugar

½ teaspoon lemon juice

1 teaspoon orange blossom water (see p. 25)

FOR THE NAMOURAH
400 g (14 oz) coarse semolina

150 g (5 oz) ghee or unsalted butter

1 tablespoon dried milk (optional)

200 g (7 oz) desiccated coconut

75 g (3 oz) caster sugar

75 ml (3 fl oz) orange blossom water

150 ml (5 fl oz) plain yoghurt

1 teaspoon bicarbonate of soda

50 g (2 oz) blanched almonds

1 tablespoon tahini (for cake tin)

TEMPERATURE
preheat the oven to gas mark 3, 325°F (170°C)

YOU WILL ALSO NEED
a 23 cm (9 inch) spring form cake tin, greased with 1 tablespoon of tahini

Express passion cake

SERVES: **6–8**

PREPARATION TIME: **20 minutes**

COOKING TIME: **30 minutes (plus
allow 2 hours cooling time for
the cake before filling)**

FOR THE CAKE MIXTURE
275 g (10 oz) self-raising flour, sifted

1 level teaspoon baking powder

½ teaspoon salt

175 g (7 oz) light soft brown sugar

½ teaspoon cinnamon

½ teaspoon freshly grated nutmeg

110 g (4 oz) carrots, peeled
and grated

1 ripe banana, peeled and mashed
with 1 tablespoon lemon juice

3 eggs, separated

½ teaspoon vanilla extract

grated rind of 1 orange

50 g (2 oz) pineapple crush, tinned or
fresh (optional)

1 tablespoon date syrup or treacle

75 g (3 oz) walnuts, coarsely chopped

150 ml (5 fl oz) corn oil

FOR THE FILLING AND TOPPING
50 g (2 oz) unsalted butter

110 g (4 oz) icing sugar, sifted

½ teaspoon lemon juice

75 g (3 oz) mascarpone

200 g (7 oz) cream cheese

50 g (2 oz) pistachio nuts,
finely chopped

*This is my all-time favourite and most useful cake. It is good to show off with
as it looks elaborate and as if a lot of hard work has gone into it, when
truthfully it is one of the easiest cakes to make. The filling and icing are the
only fiddly bits, but as they enhance the end result so greatly, it is well worth
the effort. Fatless sponges can be boring, but this cake emphasises the fact
that a cake can be light and creamy as well as healthy. As for calories, I
like to think of a slice of this cake as a slice of energy food, especially if it is
eaten for breakfast, as a snack for an empty stomach, or as a reward after
a hard day's work.*

TO MAKE THE CAKE
1 In a large bowl, put the flour, baking powder, salt, sugar, cinnamon,
   nutmeg, carrots, mashed banana, egg yolks, vanilla, orange rind,
   pineapple crush (if using), date syrup, chopped walnuts and corn oil
   and mix together well using a metal spoon.

2 Whisk the egg whites to soft peaks and fold gently into the mixture.

3 Divide the mixture evenly between the two cake tins and bake for
   15–20 minutes. When light brown, test the cake by piercing it with a
   toothpick. If the toothpick comes out dry and clean, the cake is ready.
   (The two cakes may be ready at slightly different times.)

4 Take the cakes out of the oven, allow to stand for a few minutes and
   turn them out while still warm – this will make it easier. Cool for at
   least 2 hours before filling and icing.

TO MAKE THE FILLING AND TOPPING
5 In a bowl, mix together the butter and icing sugar, followed by the
   lemon juice, and blend.

6 Add the mascarpone and cream cheese and mix to form a very light
   cream.

7 Sandwich together the two cake halves with half the filling. Then
   spread the remainder over the top of the cake. Scatter with the
   pistachios and serve.

TIPS
*   This cake can be baked in a 22 cm (9 inch) spring form tin without the
    filling and topping, allowing more time for baking (30–40 minutes).

- The cake should be kept in the refrigerator, preferably covered – for example, with a glass bowl over the top.

- Chill the filling in the refrigerator while the cakes are cooling.

- Ground walnuts can be sprinkled over at the end instead of pistachios if you prefer.

TEMPERATURE
preheat the oven to gas mark 4,
350°F (180°C)

YOU WILL ALSO NEED
2 sandwich tins, 20.5 cm (8 inch)
(preferably non-stick), greased and
dusted lightly with flour

Orange semolina cake

The recipe for this cake came about by accident. I had to make a cake quickly but did not have enough flour; hence the semolina. The combination proved to be fantastic: the result a light, orange flavoured sponge that can be eaten cold with a cup of tea or coffee, or warmed and served with a little cream. It can be a pudding or even a luxurious snack.

SERVES: **6–8**
PREPARATION TIME: **15 minutes**
COOKING TIME: **30 minutes**

3 eggs, separated

175 g (6 oz) caster sugar

100 g (4 oz) unsalted butter

1 teaspoon vanilla extract

juice and rind of 2 oranges

110 g (4 oz) self-raising flour

1 teaspoon baking powder

110 g (4 oz) semolina

50 g (2 oz) desiccated coconut

50 g (2 oz) ground almonds

TEMPERATURE
preheat the oven to gas mark 4,
350°F (180°C)

YOU WILL ALSO NEED
a greased 20 cm (8 inch) spring form
tin, greased with butter and dusted
with flour

1 Whisk the egg whites until the soft peak stage.

2 Cream the sugar and butter. Add the egg yolks and vanilla extract and beat until pale and fluffy.

3 Add the orange rind and mix well.

4 Sift the flour, baking powder and semolina into the egg mixture. Also add the coconut and almonds.

5 Mix together, and gradually add the orange juice.

6 Fold in the egg white mixture using a metal spoon.

7 Put into the tin and bake for 30 minutes.

8 When cooked the top should be a golden brown colour and when tested with a skewer or toothpick it should come out clean and dry.

9 The cake can be eaten hot with ice cream or double cream, or cold with tea or coffee.

TIP

- The most essential part of the preparation is the creaming of the sugar and butter followed by the eggs. An electric mixer is a great asset, and can be used to prepare the egg whites too.

Usmalliyeh

This is a refined version of the famous kinafah. *Capturing an authentic* kinafah *taste away from its country of origin is a difficult task because it contains ingredients that are not widely available. In making my version of this recipe accessible to everyone, I have used ingredients that can easily be obtained.*

TO PREPARE THE PASTRY

1 Take the pastry out of the packet and separate the *kataifi* by hand, easing apart the strands of pastry. Arrange half of the pastry tidily and tightly in the cake tin. Press hard.

2 Pour the corn oil over the *kataifi* pastry to soak it. Then using a masher or heavy utensil, press the pastry down as much as you can.

3 Put the cake tin on the hob on a moderate to low heat. Press the pastry down while it is lightly browning. Tilt the cake tin so that the hot oil colours the pastry evenly. This takes 15 minutes or so.

4 Once the pastry is browned evenly, tip the remaining corn oil out of the tin into the heatproof jug and turn the pastry out onto a plate to cool.

5 Wash the cake tin and strain the oil into the jug, and re-use it in repeating the process with the other half of the pastry. Add a little more corn oil if necessary, but give it a chance to heat through on the hob before adding this extra oil.

6 Cool both halves of pastry for at least 2 hours before adding the filling.

TO MAKE THE FILLING

7 Using a food processor, pulse the ricotta cheese with the sugar and orange blossom water. Transfer the mixture to a clean bowl.

8 Spread the filling on one half of the pastry, and then make a sandwich with the other half of pastry.

9 Serve sprinkled with pistachio nuts and cold *Syrup* on the side ready to drizzle over. Have a sharp knife on hand to cut into slices.

TIPS
• You will need a sharp knife to slice the *Usmalliyeh*.

SERVES: **6–8**

PREPARATION TIME: **30 minutes**

COOKING TIME: **40 minutes**

350 g (12 oz) of a packet of *kataifi* pastry (see p. 24)

325 ml (12 fl oz) corn oil

FOR THE FILLING

350 g (12 oz) ricotta cheese

50 g (2 oz) caster sugar

25 ml (1 fl oz) orange blossom water (see p. 25)

TO SERVE

110 ml (4 fl oz) cold *Syrup* (see pp. 45–6)

1 tablespoon ground pistachio nuts

YOU WILL ALSO NEED

21 x 5 cm (8 x 2 inches) deep cake tin (a *tarte tatin* tin is ideal, as you need a tin that can be heated directly on the hob)

a potato masher

a heatproof glass jug

- The colour of the pastry should be light caramel brown all over. To achieve this you will need to be patient in turning the tin and tipping the oil over while it is browning.

- *Usmalliyeh* can be eaten cold or it can be heated for a minute or so once the syrup and nuts have been added and then served immediately, which is just as delicious!

- The cake can be decorated with more filling or fruit, but I prefer it plain as it is crunchier and rich enough already.

Filo parcels

Shua'ibiyat

PREPARATION TIME: **25 minutes**

COOKING TIME: **15 minutes**

FOR THE SYRUP

225 g (8 oz) granulated sugar

150 ml (5 fl oz) water

1 teaspoon lemon juice

1 teaspoon orange blossom water (see p. 25)

FOR THE FILLING

275 ml (½ pint) full-cream milk

50 g (2 oz) caster sugar

1 tablespoon orange blossom water

50 g (2 oz) fine semolina

FOR THE PASTRY

10 sheets filo pastry (if frozen, defrosted overnight in the refrigerator)

75 g (3 oz) melted butter ghee or clarified butter

25 g (1 oz) ground pistachio nuts

This probably is one of the easiest sweet pastry desserts that can be prepared with minimum effort and guaranteed results. It can also be served straight away unlike other syrup pastries. For Ramadan it is perfect for after the meal or for snacking as it consists of fairly rich ingredients. The parcels are well worth the value of the calories however, as they melt in the mouth when eaten hot from the oven and behave well on reheating.

TO MAKE THE SYRUP

1 In a saucepan put the sugar, water, lemon juice and orange blossom water. Mix together and bring to the boil, then simmer for 10 minutes. Switch off the heat.

TO MAKE THE FILLING

2 Heat the milk in a pan, add the sugar and orange blossom water and allow to reach boiling point. As the milk starts to boil add the semolina quickly and stir. When it thickens (which will only take a few seconds), quickly pour the mixture into the pyrex dish. Allow to cool while you prepare the pastry.

TO PREPARE THE PASTRY

3 Take one sheet of filo pastry and lay it on a board. Brush all over with the melted ghee or clarified butter, add another sheet of filo on top

and brush with more melted ghee or butter. Repeat with the rest of the sheets leaving the last sheet of filo free of butter.

4 Using a sharp knife cut the pastry into 7 cm (2.8 inch) squares.

5 Put one teaspoon of the filling in the middle of each square, fold over into a triangle and brush generously all over with melted ghee or butter.

6 Brush the baking tray with melted ghee or butter and transfer the prepared pastries neatly on to it. Repeat with the second tray.

7 Transfer the trays to the oven and bake for 10 minutes until the pastry turns light brown.

8 Take out of the oven and pour some of the syrup on the tray. Let the pastries soak it up before you add more. Leave the pastries for a few minutes and serve while still hot, sprinkled with the ground pistachio nuts.

TIPS

• The filo sheets should be covered with a damp cloth while you are preparing the pastry as they dry up very quickly.

• Do not be tempted to overfill the triangles as they will overspill and burn in the oven while baking.

• When you fold over the ends of the pastries just press lightly, then brush with ghee. They will seal on baking.

• The pastries behave well on reheating as a great snack, especially mid-morning.

TEMPERATURE
preheat the oven to gas mark 6, 400°F (220°C)

YOU WILL ALSO NEED
pastry brush

2 baking trays, 15 x 21 cm (6 x 8 inches)

275 ml (½ pint) capacity flat Pyrex dish

MAKES: 25 medium-sized pieces
PREPARATION TIME: 40 minutes
COOKING TIME: 10 minutes plus proving time of 1 hour

FOR THE DOUGH
150 g (5 oz) fine semolina

110 g (4 oz) coarse semolina

15 g (½ oz) icing sugar

1 teaspoon active dried yeast

90 g (3½ oz) ghee or unsalted butter at room temperature

40 ml (1½ fl oz) rose water

75 ml (3 fl oz) orange blossom water (see p. 25)

FOR THE FILLING
200 g (7 oz) date paste (widely available in Middle Eastern shops)

1 teaspoon orange blossom water

40 g (1½ oz) unsalted butter

TEMPERATURE
preheat the oven to gas mark 6, 400°F (200°C)

YOU WILL ALSO NEED
a baking tray lined with baking parchment

ma'amoul mould, available in speciality shops and Middle Eastern grocers (optional)

a polythene bag

Date cookies

One of the easiest and most rewarding Lebanese pastries is Ma'amoul. It does not take any longer to prepare than a cake, and the outcome is delicious. I think shop-bought Ma'amoul is good but home-made is better, and once you have mastered it there are many different fillings to experiment with.

1 In a large bowl mix the fine and coarse semolina followed by the icing sugar, yeast and ghee or butter and blend together by hand until the ghee or butter is totally absorbed by the semolina. Pour in the rose water and mix to form a dough. Then add a few drops of the orange blossom water. Put the dough in the polythene bag and allow to stand for 1 hour.

2 Meanwhile, heat the date paste for a few minutes to soften it, mix in the rest of the orange blossom water and butter, blend together and set aside.

3 Form small balls of 1½ cm (¾ inch) from the date paste mixture and set aside on a plate.

4 Take the dough out of the polythene bag, wet the palms of your hands with orange blossom water, and form dough balls of 3 cm (1.2 inches) in diameter.

5 Take one of the dough balls and using your forefinger, make a hole for the filling. Put one ball of the date paste mixture in the cavity, seal gently and form back into a ball, wetting your hands with the orange blossom water. Gently transfer to the baking tray.

6 If you have a mould, you can put the sealed, stuffed dough ball into it and press it in gently to form a shape. Transfer to the baking tray gently and repeat with the rest of the dough balls.

7 Place the baking tray on the highest shelf of the oven for 8–10 minutes and keep a close eye on the cookies. When cooked they should be light brown.

8 Take out, cool on a tray, transfer to a serving dish and reward yourself.

TIPS
• The dough should pliable and not dry throughout.
• The date paste should be soft and not sticky.

- The oven temperature is as important as the position of the tray in the oven. Try to be very accurate, and watch the cookies through the glass door while baking.
- The cookies can be stored for at least 3 weeks in an airtight tin.

Ma'amoul bil fostoc

MAKES ABOUT: **28–30 *Ma'amouls***
PREPARATION TIME: **30 minutes**
PROVING TIME: **1 hour 35 minutes**
COOKING TIME: **15 minutes**

FOR THE DOUGH
350 g (12 oz) fine semolina
225 g (8 oz) unsalted butter
½ teaspoon sugar
1 teaspoon active dried yeast
2 tablespoons orange blossom water (see p. 25)
50 ml (2 fl oz) milk

FOR THE FILLING
150 g (5 oz) coarsely minced pistachio nuts (for best results process in a food processor using the pulse motion until required texture is reached)
2 oz (50 g) granulated sugar
1 tablespoon orange blossom water

TO FINISH
icing sugar for dusting

Pistachio cookies

This is another version of Ma'amoul, one of the real favourites in the Middle East as it is the main sweet offered during the festivities whether for the Eid or Easter, Christmas or any festive occasion.

1 In a large bowl place the semolina, butter and sugar and rub together with your fingertips.

2 Allow to rest for an hour then add the yeast, orange blossom water and the milk. Knead the dough and allow to rest for a further 30 minutes. Knead thereafter for 5 minutes to bind together.

3 Mix all the filling ingredients in a small bowl.

4 Take one tablespoon of the dough into your hand and shape into a ball. Make a hole in the centre creating a cavity for the filling. Fill with 1 teaspoon of filling, seal firmly and then place the shape into the mould. Press gently to form the shape then knock it against the board to release from the mould. Transfer to the baking tray, leaving a gap of 2 cms (1 inch) between the cookies.

5 Repeat with the rest of the *Ma'amouls* until the dough and filling are finished.

6 Place the baking trays in the preheated oven for 15 minutes or until golden brown.

7 Allow to cool for 5 minutes on the trays, then sprinkle generously with icing sugar and store when cold in an airtight container. *Eid sae'ed* as we say in Arabic!

TIPS

- The proving time is vital to the required result, as it ensures that the texture of the cookies is light yet perfectly combined.

- If a mould is not available, shape the filled dough into a cylinder and then using the tip of a fork press down to create a pattern.

- Walnuts can be used for an alternative filling instead of the pistachios. Also add ½ teaspoon of ground cinnamon.

- Do not over-bake the cookies as they become hard quickly – watch for that light golden colour.

- If a less sweet version is required omit the icing sugar in the end and serve without, just as delicious.

- "Practice makes perfect": remember this saying if your first attempt is not to the required standard. The making of *Ma'amoul* is very therapeutic once the technique is mastered. Be patient!

TEMPERATURE
preheat the oven to gas mark 7, 425°F (220°C)

YOU WILL ALSO NEED
cling film for covering the dough

ma'amoul mould, available in speciality shops and Middle Eastern grocers (optional)

2 baking trays

BREAD AND PIZZAS

I enjoy making bread. I find it very therapeutic. But many people are frightened that they'll get it wrong, and others may feel it's just too much trouble. It's true, bread-making is not for everyone. However, I feel I should include it in this book to give those interested an idea of the procedure involved in creating the basic dough. Once you have this dough, you have pittas, *Halabis* and pizzas – and that's just to start with. I urge you to give it a go. I'm sure you'll find the effort very rewarding.

Basic dough

This recipe provides the ingredients and method for the basic dough mixture from which you can make pitta breads (see pp. 211–12), Halabi (pp. 212–13) and pizzas (pp. 213–21). So it is worth familiarising yourself with it and once you've had a chance to study it, I'm sure you'll agree it's not at all complicated.

MAKES: **this dough mix will make 36 pittas or 6 large *Halabi***

PREPARATION TIME: **10 minutes**

PROVING TIME: **50 minutes**

750 g (1 lb 8oz) plain flour, sifted

6 g sachet active dried yeast or 1 teaspoon fresh yeast

2 tablespoons granulated sugar

1½ tablespoons salt

300 ml (15 fl oz) lukewarm water

1 Put the flour, yeast, sugar and salt into a food processor and process for a minute or so.

2 Through the feed tube add the water slowly and carefully until you have a ball of dough.

3 Take out the dough and knead a little. Put in a bowl, cover with cling film and a tea towel and put in a warm place to prove for 50 minutes to an hour. Reduce the proving time to half an hour if fresh yeast is used.

4 You now have a batch of basic dough mix to use however you decide.

TIPS

- Fresh yeast gives a better result as it is quicker to prove the dough and it creates a lighter textured bread. Add 1 teaspoon of fresh yeast to the lukewarm water, blend to mix and add to the flour through the feed tube. Continue with the rest of the recipe as above, reducing the proving time to 30 minutes.

- The water used should not be hot or cold, but lukewarm. Increase the temperature slightly during the winter as cold weather will affect the proving.

- A dough machine is just as good as if not better than using a food processor, so use it if you have one.

- You might not need to use all the water, or you might need a little more than stated above; some flours are drier than others. Just make sure that the dough forms a ball leaving no residue in the food processor.

Pitta bread

Pitta bread is the most basic accompaniment to any Lebanese dish, whether it is a starter or a main course, salad or snack. The many varieties that are available in the shops are a good enough reason not to encourage making it at home. But it is nice to know that you can make it, if an emergency arises. Remember that making bread is very therapeutic and enhancing to the spirit, and is very enjoyable. Please have a go, it is a challenge worth taking on.

1 Once the basic dough is made, divide before proving. Cut the basic dough into 3 portions with a sharp knife. Take one portion to work with and cover the other two with cling film until needed.

2 Roll one portion into a sausage shape between the palm of your hand and the board.

3 Cut the cylinder into 8 pieces with a sharp knife and roll each piece into a ball.

4 Put the 8 balls to one side covered with a damp cloth while you prepare the other 2 portions of basic dough in the same way.

5 When all the balls are ready, take them one by one and dust them lightly with flour. Shake off some of the flour and roll them into a circle 7.5 cm (3 inches) in diameter.

6 Lay the dough circles on the trays. Brush off the excess flour using a pastry brush. Cover each tray with a damp cloth while you prepare the rest of the balls.

7 Allow the dough circles to rest on the covered trays for a least half an hour to an hour.

8 Transfer a batch of the pittas carefully to the oven tray and bake for 1–2 minutes, keeping a close eye on them. When they are cooked, a dome-like shape will be created. Take out and allow to cool, or serve immediately.

9 Repeat with the rest of the pittas.

TIPS
- Place the oven tray at a low level in the oven.
- Do not be tempted to put more than one tray at a time in the oven, as the bread needs a lot of heat to rise and bake quickly without drying.

MAKES: **24 pittas**

PREPARATION TIME: **20 minutes after preparation of the basic dough (see p. 210)**

COOKING TIME: **12 minutes**

basic dough (see p. 210)

75 g (3 oz) plain flour for assembling the dough

TEMPERATURE
preheat the oven to gas mark 9, 475°F (240°C)

YOU WILL ALSO NEED
4 baking trays lined with baking parchment

cling film or 4 damp tea towels

a small pastry brush

rolling pin

- Handle the unbaked bread with great care, as if the edges of the dough circles are dented, the bread will not rise.

- When you roll the dough balls, use a round, even motion to create an even surface for rising.

- The pittas can be enjoyed hot, or once cooled, they can be put in freezer bags and frozen and reheated when required.

Halabi bread

MAKES: **6 Halabi**

PREPARATION TIME: **20 minutes after preparation of the basic dough (see p. 210)**

COOKING TIME: **6–8 minutes**

Half quantity of basic dough (p. 210)

50 g (2 oz) plain flour to assemble

YOU WILL ALSO NEED

3 baking trays lined with baking parchment

2 damp tea towels or cling film

pastry brush

a griddle preheated for 10 minutes

This bread was named after the baker at my restaurant, as he created this special bread. As he came originally from Halab (Aleppo) in Syria, we called the bread Halabi after him. It is great bread, lighter than pitta, and not a lot of proving is required. It needs a powerful oven to really puff the dough up, and the bread is soft as well as light. I have devised this domestic approach, whereby the bread is more like a wrap, with the same effect of lightness, but more versatile to cope with the pressures of modern busy life. It can be used for sandwiches, toasted for soups, and it is needed for various recipes, for example Mousakhan and Mansaf. You will find you will have plenty of usages for it. It is easy to master, and once made it can be stored in a polythene bag in the refrigerator and keeps well for 5–6 days. It can be frozen if necessary, and once defrosted and reheated, it is as if freshly baked.

1 Knead the prepared *Basic dough* lightly and roll into a sausage shape. Cut the dough into 6 pieces with a sharp knife.

2 Roll each piece into a ball. Dip one side in flour, put aside and cover with a damp cloth.

3 Take each ball, flour the rolling pin and roll into a circle with a diameter of roughly 20 cm (8 inches).

4 Brush the excess flour off the dough circles. Place on the tray and cover with cling film or a damp cloth, until they are all finished.

5 Transfer the circles one by one to the heated griddle. Turn the heat to very low and, using gloves, press the dough down so it does not rise.

Cook until the dough browns slightly and turn over. This will take less than one minute.

6 Allow to cool on a tray, then fold and put into a polythene bag to store in the refrigerator until required.

TIPS

- Make sure there is enough flour on the board while rolling the dough, as it helps greatly, but then make sure you shake off the excess by using a pastry brush.

- The griddle should be wiped with a wet cloth between cooking each *Halabi* to remove excess flour.

- *Halabi* bread is extremely versatile, it is more like a wrap and is especially used to cover grills so that they do not dry out, or cut into square small pieces and browned under the grill to make croutons for soup or *Fattoush* salad, or simply used as a sandwich wrap for *Falafel* or any other sandwich.

- When you roll the dough balls, always use a round motion to create even surfaces so that the dough cooks evenly.

Lebanese pizza

Lahem bil ageine *is the Lebanese pizza. It is famous all over the Middle East because it is the most typical snack. Its mild ingredients are what make it popular. The base is similar to standard pizza, but the topping is the main distinction.* Lahem bil ageine *is normally served with yoghurt, or as part of the Lebanese mezze, to eat with dips and salads.*

TO PREPARE THE TOPPING

1 In bowl mix the onion, salt, pepper and cinnamon. Then add the minced meat followed by the tomatoes and olive oil. Mix well, then transfer to a colander to squeeze out any excess liquid.

2 Put the mixture back in the bowl and add the pomegranate syrup. Taste and adjust accordingly, cover with cling film and chill in the refrigerator until needed.

Lahem bil ageine

MAKES: **16 small pizzas**

PREPARATION TIME: **40 minutes after preparation of the basic dough (see p. 210)**

COOKING TIME: **10 minutes**

FOR THE BASE
Half quantity of basic dough (p. 210)

75 g (3 oz) plain flour

FOR THE TOPPING
1 onion, peeled and chopped

1 teaspoon salt

½ teaspoon white pepper

1 teaspoon cinnamon

110 g (4 oz) lamb, finely minced

4 beef tomatoes or 6 salad tomatoes, skinned and finely chopped

50 ml (2 fl oz) extra virgin olive oil

1 tablespoon pomegranate syrup

TEMPERATURE
preheat the oven to gas mark 8,
450°F (230°C)

YOU WILL ALSO NEED
4 baking trays lined with
baking parchment

rolling pin

damp tea towel or cling film

TO ACCOMPANY
yoghurt and olives

TO PREPARE THE BASE

3 Divide the dough into 16 balls cover with a damp cloth.

4 Dip each ball into the flour. Roll out each dough ball into a circle 10 cm (4 inches) in diameter. Shake the excess flour from each circle and put on one of the trays lined with baking parchment. Cover the trays with cling film as you go along, to prevent the dough from drying out.

5 Form an edge around each circle and tap the middle, to stop the dough from rising there.

TO ASSEMBLE

6 Remove the cling film and put 1½ tablespoons of the topping on each circle. Allow to rest for 10 minutes or so to create the edge round the filling.

TO COOK

7 Place on a baking tray and cook each batch on the middle shelf of the oven for 2–3 minutes. Check that both the dough and filling are cooked.

8 Repeat procedure with all the pizzas.

TO SERVE

9 Allow to cool for a few minutes, and serve with the suggested accompaniments.

TIPS

- Proving the dough circles with the topping is optional but gives a better result.

- Make sure that the dough circles have an edge, and that their centres are flattened before spooning on the filling.

- Dip your fingertips in a bit of olive oil when tapping the circles to flatten them, ready for the filling.

- Keep the trays covered with cling film throughout the preparation, so as to keep the dough from drying out.

- Spread the topping gently in the middle of the circles without touching the edges.

- When rolling out the dough, do it in a circular even motion as this improves the presentation.

MAKES: **16 Sfeihas**

PREPARATION TIME: **40 minutes after preparation of the basic dough (see p. 210)**

COOKING TIME: **20 minutes**

FOR THE BASE

Half quantity of basic dough (p. 210)

75 g (3 oz) flour

FOR THE TOPPING

110 g (4 oz) lamb, finely minced

1 medium onion, peeled and very finely chopped

1 teaspoon salt

½ teaspoon white pepper

½ teaspoon cinnamon

½ teaspoon ground allspice

½ teaspoon freshly grated nutmeg

½ red pepper, deseeded and very finely chopped

1 tablespoon fresh parsley, very finely chopped

2 cloves garlic, peeled and very finely chopped

3 beef tomatoes, skinned and puréed

50 ml (2 fl oz) extra virgin olive oil

1 tablespoon pomegranate syrup

1 tablespoon *Red chilli sauce* (see pp. 38–9)

TEMPERATURE

preheat the oven to gas mark 8, 450°F (230°C)

YOU WILL ALSO NEED

4 baking trays lined with baking parchment

rolling pin

cling film or a damp tea towel

216

Spicy pizza

Sfeiha *is a spicy pizza which originally came from Armenia, but which has been altered into a milder form. It is for the adventurous. You can cool down its spicy flavour by serving it with* Yoghurt cheese *(see p. 76) or* Perfect hommous *(see p. 66). It is a great accompaniment to mezze and is especially versatile for parties. It tastes good hot or cold, and behaves well on reheating.*

TO PREPARE THE TOPPING

1 Mix the meat, onion, salt, pepper, cinnamon, allspice, nutmeg, red pepper, parsley, garlic, tomatoes and olive oil in a bowl. Transfer the mixture to a colander and squeeze out any liquid.

2 Put the mixture back in the bowl. Add the pomegranate syrup and *Red chilli sauce*. Adjust the seasoning as required. Cover with cling film and chill in the refrigerator until required.

TO PREPARE THE BASE

3 See *Lebanese pizza* recipe, pp. 213–14. Follow it up to stage 4 inclusive.

TO COOK

4 Transfer a circle of dough to the heated griddle and add 1 tablespoon of filling, spreading it all over without spilling over the edges.

5 Have the tray lined with parchment ready. Put 4 *Sfeiha*s on the tray, transfer to the heated oven and bake for 1–2 minutes checking regularly through the oven window. The *Sfeiha*s are ready when the top of them are light brown and the topping is cooked.

6 Can be served with *Yoghurt cheese* or *Perfect hommous*.

TIPS

* The best way to eat *Sfeiha* is to roll it up and dip it in the yoghurt or *hommous*: therefore don't be tempted to overload the topping.

* Smaller sized *Sfeiha*s can be made by rolling the dough and using a ring cutter to the required size, and then topped. Great for parties.

* *Sfeiha*s freeze well. Once cooled divide into small batches, put in freezer bags and put carefully in a drawer in the freezer compartment. Defrost when needed, preferably overnight in the refrigerator, or by keeping the bag out for few hours. Reheat in a warm oven and serve.

Cheese pizza

Kallaj *is a cheese pizza that is rich in flavour and content. It is popular for breakfast or a light lunch, washed down with mint tea. Once prepared and baked it should ideally be served straight away, as the halloumi topping does not respond well to reheating.*

TO PREPARE THE BASE

1 See *Lebanese pizza* recipe, pp. 213–14. Follow up to stage 4 inclusive.

TO ASSEMBLE

2 Place 3 or 4 slices of halloumi on each dough circle, making sure there are no gaps. Brush lightly with olive oil and sprinkle with dried mint or thyme.

3 Repeat with all the dough circles.

TO COOK

4 Place on the baking trays and cook in batches, one tray at a time, for 2–3 minutes until the cheese melts and the base is cooked. Keep a close eye on them.

TO SERVE

5 Serve immediately with slices of cucumber, tomato, olives and sprigs of fresh mint.

TIPS

- Do not be tempted to put more than one tray at a time in the heated oven.
- The cheese should be sliced very thinly to cover the dough completely while it is still able to cook.
- Instead of sprinkling mint on to the cooked pizza, you can sprinkle on thyme.
- Halloumi is the best kind of cheese to use as it provides richness and a distinctive flavour.

Kallaj

MAKES: 16

PREPARATION TIME: 1 hour, including preparation of the basic dough (see p. 210)

COOKING TIME: 10–12 minutes

FOR THE BASE
Half quantity of basic dough (p. 210)

FOR THE TOPPING
500 g (16 oz) (2 blocks) halloumi cheese, washed, dried and thinly sliced

50 ml (2 fl oz) extra virgin olive oil for brushing over cheese

1 teaspoon dried mint or thyme

TO GARNISH
1 cucumber, sliced

sliced tomatoes

green and black olives

sprigs of fresh mint

TEMPERATURE
preheat the oven to gas mark 8, 450°F (230°C)

YOU WILL ALSO NEED
4 baking trays, lined with baking parchment

rolling pin

pastry brush

Manakeesh biza'atar

Manakeesh are eaten at all times, and are a firm favourite with everyone. They are heavenly, especially when accompanied by yoghurt, sliced tomatoes, sliced cucumbers and black olives; this is the typical luxurious Lebanese breakfast, which could extend through to brunch, lunch and thereafter.

It took me few attempts to achieve this now foolproof method, which I think is the best approach to making Manakeesh at home. Please stick to the amounts given for the topping as burning the topping while cooking the perfect base can be very frustrating.

MAKES: 16

PREPARATION TIME: 20 minutes after preparation of the basic dough (see p. 210)

COOKING TIME: 10 minutes

FOR THE BASE

Half quantity of basic dough (p. 210)

FOR THE TOPPING

2 tablespoons chopped fresh thyme

50 ml (2 fl oz) extra virgin olive oil

TEMPERATURE

preheat the grill to a medium heat

YOU WILL ALSO NEED

4 baking trays lined with baking parchment

rolling pin

damp tea towel or cling film

a griddle preheated for 10 minutes

TO ACCOMPANY

Yoghurt cheese (see p. 76), sliced tomatoes, sliced cucumbers and olives

TO PREPARE THE BASE

1 As for *Lebanese pizza*, pp. 213–14. Follow up to stage 4 inclusive.

TO PREPARE THE TOPPING

2 In a bowl, mix the thyme with the olive oil.

TO COOK

3 Transfer a circle of dough to the griddle, make sure the heat is low and spread the topping all over leaving an edge of ½ cm.

4 Cook the dough for 1 minute, and then transfer to the tray lined with baking parchment.

5 Repeat with more dough circles until the tray is full. Then place the tray under the oven grill for 1 minute or so, making sure that the topping and dough are very light brown, making sure they do not burn.

6 Take out of the oven. Repeat the procedure with the rest of the dough circles.

7 Serve with the suggested accompaniments.

TIPS

- Mix the thyme and oil before preparing the dough so that it gives the ingredients the chance to enhance each others' flavours.

- A heavy non-stick pan can be used instead of a griddle, following the same method.

- Do not be tempted to increase the amount of topping. If anything using less topping gives you a better result.

Arayes

Another very practical version of Lebanese pizzas is Arayes. It is a version using Kafta halabiyeh *and is drizzled with tahini sauce, which enhances the kafta immensely and adds creaminess and richness to it. It is very different from other pizzas, and is especially popular with kids, and ideal for birthday parties and buffets.*

1 Follow the *Lebanese pizza* recipe on pp. 213–14 up to stage 4, inclusive.

2 Put 1½ tablespoons of the *Lamb kebabs* mixture (see p. 183) on the prepared dough base, drizzle with a little *Tahini sauce* and sprinkle over a few pine nuts. Repeat with the rest of the dough circles.

3 Bake for 2–3 minutes in the preheated oven and repeat with the rest of the dough circles.

4 Serve and enjoy accompanied with various dips and salads. Yoghurt is a particular favourite with this dish.

TIPS

- This recipe is ideal if you have left over *kafta* in the refrigerator that needs to be used.
- For a party, double the amounts.
- Be generous with the topping, but not with the *Tahini sauce* as it may spill out and burn.

MAKES: **16**

PREPARATION TIME: **40 minutes after preparation of the basic dough (see p. 210)**

COOKING TIME: **10–12 minutes**

FOR THE BASE
Half quantity of basic dough (p. 210)

FOR THE TOPPING
110 g (4 oz) *Kafta halabiyeh* mixture (see p. 183)

50 ml (2 fl oz) *Tahini sauce* (see p. 47)

50 g (2 oz) pine nuts

TEMPERATURE
preheat the oven to gas mark 8, 450°F (230°C)

Sfeiha ba'albakiyeh

This is definitely the richest Lebanese pizza you can make, and it certainly is not for dieters. So make it when you need a real treat and calories are not an issue. The whole process of making it is very simple but I don't know why every time I make it I am left with this guilty feeling that prevents me from enjoying the result... This pizza can be frozen after it is baked and cooled and once reheated is as good as fresh.

1 In a large bowl mix the flour, yeast and ghee and work the dough using your fingertips until it resembles breadcrumbs. Add the salt and gradually the lukewarm water until a dough is formed.

MAKES: **16**

PREPARATION TIME: **30 minutes**

PROVING TIME: **15 minutes**

COOKING TIME: **15 minutes**

FOR THE BASE
350 g (12 oz) plain flour, sifted

½ teaspoon active dried yeast

75 g (3 oz) vegetable ghee

2 Place the dough in a polythene bag and allow to rest for 15 minutes.

3 To prepare the topping, in another bowl mix the mince, onion, tomatoes, salt, pepper, cinnamon, yoghurt, pomegranate syrup and pine nuts and mix thoroughly.

4 Form a cylinder with the dough and cut into circles. Take a circle and using the palm of your hand form into a ball.

5 Brush the surface that you are working on with ghee or melted butter and using the fingertips spread out the dough to form a square. Brush the square with ghee and then fold the ends to form a hexagon shape. Transfer the shape to the greased baking tray, and brush with ghee. Repeat with the rest of the circles.

6 Cover the base with topping leaving a small margin so it doesn't overflow onto the baking tray. Repeat with the rest of the pizza bases until the filling is finished.

7 Place the trays in the preheated oven and bake for about 12–15 minutes until the pizzas are a light golden brown.

8 Serve the pizzas on a large platter decorated with lemon wedges, parsley and mint sprigs.

TIPS

- The process might sound complicated but once you follow the steps it all falls into place.
- Oven temperatures vary so watch the oven and feel free to decrease or increase the baking time until the required result is achieved.
- Lean lamb mince is a must otherwise the result is not as tasty.
- The dough can be proven at room temperature, but allow more time during the very cold winter months.

1 teaspoon salt

50 ml (2 fl oz) lukewarm water

2 tablespoons vegetable ghee (or unsalted butter at room temperature) for brushing over the dough

FOR THE TOPPING
350 g (12 oz) lean lamb mince

1 onion, peeled and finely chopped

2 beef tomatoes or 3 salad tomatoes, finely chopped

1 teaspoon salt

½ teaspoon white pepper

½ teaspoon cinnamon

75 g (3 oz) *Yoghurt cheese* (see p. 76) or Greek yoghurt

1 tablespoon pomegranate syrup

50 g (2 oz) pine nuts

TO SERVE
lemon wedges

sprigs of fresh parsley and mint

TEMPERATURE
preheat the oven to gas mark 2, 300°F (150°C)

YOU WILL ALSO NEED
a large polythene bag

2 baking trays greased with ghee or butter

a pastry brush

DRINKS

Hot drinks, usually coffee, play a very important part in the Lebanese way of life. Summer and winter do not alter this aspect of social life. This can be very demanding for the host at times, as the coffee kettle does not take a break, and every household has to have at least three or four different sized coffee kettles to cope with demand and the different number of cups required. Arabic coffee is very much part of the cuisine – you would never go without Arabic coffee after a Lebanese meal! Another important coffee-drinking time is mid-morning.

Tea is consumed but not as often as coffee, and mostly during the winter months. Mint tea is the version that commonly accompanies a meal. As for other types of drinks, lemonade is a very popular summer drink, and a date syrup drink (*Jallab*) is popular on festive occasions or during Ramadan – the fasting month. The apricot drink (*Kamardin*) is another energiser for the fasting month as it helps the body cope with the immense digestive pressure that is inflicted on the system during Ramadan. The yoghurt drink (*Laban e'ran*) is very popular at meal times as it supposedly helps with the process of digestion.

I hope my selection will help to give you an idea about some of the simple beverages of Lebanese cuisine. They are all simple to prepare and very readily available. They can be healthy and nutritious if consumed reasonably and not excessively.

Ahwe'

SERVES: **4**

PREPARATION TIME: **10 minutes**

COOKING TIME: **5 minutes**

Arabic coffee

sugar, according to level of sweetness desired

YOU WILL ALSO NEED

a *Raqui* (coffee pot) – if not available, a small milk pan. *Raquis* are sold in Middle Eastern delicatessens and grocers throughout London. See p. 18 to find suppliers

4 espresso coffee cups and saucers

Arabic coffee

After a Lebanese meal, no matter how light or heavy, Arabic coffee has to follow. First thing in the morning strong coffee is the most popular drink, to perk one up and wake the sleepy. The Raqui or coffee pot works without a break, because elevenses, a sociable time of the day, means coffee with friends or neighbours. Coffee is also popular in the late afternoon, acting as therapy after a day's work (elsewhere in the world people are drinking tea!). Coffee is shared by the whole family, even children, who get used to the strong taste early on. It then becomes a way of life.

Arabic coffee is roasted and ground in such a way that it froths and boils quickly. Cardamom pods are roasted and ground and then added to the coffee.

It can be served in 4 ways: without sugar (sada), with a little sugar (al riha), with a medium amount of sugar (wasat) or sweet with a lot of sugar (hilweh).

FOR MEDIUM SWEET COFFEE

1 Measure 4 espresso-size cups of water into the coffee pot or small saucepan and put on a medium heat to boil.

2 When it has started boiling, add 1½ teaspoons of sugar and stir to dissolve.

3 Lower the heat and add 3 heaped teaspoons of Arabic coffee.

4 Stir and turn up the heat again until it comes to the boil.

5 Take off the heat, spoon a little of the foam which has gathered on top of the coffee into each cup, heat up again until it comes to the boil and repeat this process until the coffee has come to the boil 3 times.

6 Let the coffee settle for a few minutes before you serve it.

TO SERVE

7 Pour the coffee into the cups onto the foam spooned in previously. Arabic coffee is always served with a glass of still water with which to clear the palate before and after drinking.

TIPS

- For sweeter coffee (*hilweh*), double the amount of sugar in the recipe above.

- For slightly sweet coffee (*al riba*), just add one teaspoon of sugar.

- You don't need to use any sugar; if you don't, you will have *sada*, sugar-free coffee.

Mint tea

SERVES: **4**

PREPARATION TIME: **5 minutes**

COOKING TIME: **5 minutes**

570 ml (1 pint) water

2 tea bags or 2 teaspoons of tea leaves (Ceylon tea helps make very good mint tea)

1 heaped tablespoon of fresh mint leaves

sugar, to taste

YOU WILL ALSO NEED

ideally a metal tea pot you can put on the hob, as this will enable you to warm up the tea on a low flame before serving

4 cups, preferably glass to show off the colour of the tea

Mint tea is another very popular beverage and the main alternative to coffee. Mint is available in nearly every garden or window box, hence the pervasiveness of this tea. It is a great remedy for colds, flu and indigestion. It is thirst-quenching in the summer and warming in the winter. Sugar is normally served separately.

1 Boil the water.

2 Put the tea bags or tea leaves into a teapot, followed by the fresh mint leaves.

3 Pour in the boiling water and stir.

4 Put the teapot over a low flame and allow to simmer for a minute.

5 Cover with a tea cosy and allow to stand for a few minutes to infuse the flavour of the mint leaves.

6 Pour into the glass cups and serve with sugar on the side.

TIPS

* Tear the mint leaves before adding them to the teapot.

* A tablespoon of sugar can be added to the teapot after simmering the tea, so as to prevent the tea from becoming stronger in colour and flavour. It sweetens the tea a bit, but enhances the flavour.

* Always use a strainer when pouring the tea.

* Another version of mint tea that is particularly good for indigestion or stomach problems is made by repeatedly boiling just the mint leaves in the water to get the maximum amount of flavour and mint infusion.

Sage tea

Shai bi' mairamiyeh

This is another very popular tea. Replace the mint leaves with dried or fresh sage leaves (if available) and follow same method as for mint tea.

Camomile tea

Zhurat

Camomile tea is good tea for colds and flu and soothes all sorts of anxieties. Add two camomile teabags to the teapot. Add 570 ml (1 pint) of boiling water and simmer for a minute on low flame, allow to stand for a few minutes, covered if possible, then pour into glass cups, consume and – hopefully – recover!

Ginger tea

This tea is becoming very popular. Personally I drink it all the time. It is thirst-quenching and very mild. You can keep it in a flask so it is available at all times.

1 Peel and chop a 4 cm (1¼ inch) piece of fresh root ginger and place it in a flask or a teapot.

2 Add 570 ml (1 pint) boiling water to the flask or teapot, and allow to infuse for few minutes.

3 Serve in glass cups and get healthy!

4 Serve honey or sugar (not that you really need it) to accompany.

White coffee

Ahweh baida

White coffee is a great cleanser because it is simply a mixture of boiling water and orange blossom water. Perfect to start or end the day with. Simply pour the boiling water into the waiting cup and stir in 1 tablespoon orange blossom water per cup

Fresh lemonade

This is a very refreshing drink on a hot summer's day after a hard day's work, or to drink when relaxing in the garden. Place the ingredients in a blender and whizz for a few seconds. Serve and enjoy!

TIP
• This lemonade is best served as soon as it is made to reduce the acidity level.

Lemonada

PER PERSON
50 ml (2 fl oz) lemon juice

2 tablespoons *Syrup* (see pp. 45–6)

½ teaspoon orange blossom water (see p. 25)

½ teaspoon chopped fresh mint

2 ice cubes

150 ml (1 fl oz) chilled water

Yoghurt drink

This yoghurt drink is very good during the fasting month of Ramadan as it helps with digestion. It is also popular as a summer drink, and as an aperitif before a meal.

1 Place the ingredients in a blender, process and then pour into a glass.

2 Sprinkle with the dried mint and decorate with a few mint leaves.

TIPS
• Ice cubes can replace the water for an even more chilled version.

• The dried mint is optional but traditional.

• Any plain yoghurt can be used but the creamier the yoghurt the tastier the drink will be.

• The drink can be prepared in advance and chilled in the refrigerator for a few hours before serving.

Laban e'ran

PREPARATION TIME: 5 minutes
COOKING TIME: 50 minutes

PER PERSON
60 ml (2 fl oz) plain yoghurt

150 ml (5 fl oz) chilled water

½ teaspoon lemon juice

a little salt to taste

TO SERVE
¼ teaspoon dried mint

fresh mint leaves

1 tablespoon date syrup

230 ml (8 fl oz) chilled water
(depending on size of glasses used)

pine nuts

Date syrup drink

This is a very nutritious drink that is simple to make. Jallab is available in bottles from Middle Eastern grocers and delicatessens. It is another drink that is useful during Ramadan because of its nutritional value and energy level.

1 Mix the syrup with the water.

2 Serve with pine nuts sprinkled over.

Kamardin

SERVES: **5–6**
(makes a jug of 2 litres, 3½ pints)
PREPARATION TIME: **15 minutes**
COOKING TIME: **25 minutes plus
cooling and chilling for a
minimum of 2 hours**

500 g (17.5 oz) sheet of *kamardin* paste, broken into pieces, and placed in a large saucepan

145 g (5 oz) granulated sugar

900 ml (1½ pints) boiling water

18 ice cubes

570 ml (1 pint) chilled water

75 ml (4 fl oz) orange blossom water
(see p. 25)

Apricot drink

Kamardin is a very substantial drink and is a natural source of fibre. Once again, it is frequently drunk in Ramadan. Kamardin comes in paste form, in sheets. It is manufactured from apricots that are sieved and processed.

1 Pour the boiling water into the saucepan and mix with the broken pieces of *kamardin*.

2 Heat the saucepan on a moderate to low heat to allow the kamardin paste to dissolve in the water. Be patient as this takes about 15 minutes. Stir occasionally.

3 When the paste has fully dissolved, add the ice cubes to the saucepan to lower the temperature of the mixture.

4 Add the sugar, orange blossom water, and mix together so that the sugar dissolves.

5 Add the chilled water, mix, taste and adjust accordingly.

6 Pour the drink into a large jug, or divide into bottles, cover and when cooled, place in the refrigerator.

7 Chill the *kamardin* for a minimum of 2 hours, then serve.

TIPS
- This drink is the most important for Ramadan, as it provides one with enough nourishment to cope through the next fasting day. Ideally *kamardin* has to be prepared in the morning during Ramadan for it to be ready in time for breaking the fast.

- Do not hesitate to make the drink thinner or thicker according to personal taste.

- *Kamardin* keeps very well chilled in the refrigerator for up to a week.

INDEX

Page numbers in italics indicate photographs.